Becky Goldsmith

Sizzle Quilt

Sew 9 Paper-Pieced Stars & Appliqué Striking Borders

2 Bold Colorways

C&T PUBLISHING

Text, photography, and artwork copyright © 2020 by Becky Goldsmith

Publisher: Amy Barrett-Daffin

Creative Director: Gailen Runge

Acquisitions Editor: Roxane Cerda

Managing Editor: Liz Aneloski

Editor: Roxane Cerda

Technical Editors: Barbara Black and Julie Waldman

Cover/Book Designer: April Mostek

Production Coordinator: Tim Manibusan

Production Editor: Alice Mace Nakanishi

Illustrator: Becky Goldsmith

Quilt photography by Gregory Case Photography, courtesy of The Quilt Show; all other photography by Becky Goldsmith

Published by C&T Publishing, Inc., P.O. Box 1456, Lafayette, CA 94549

Library of Congress Control Number: 2020940828

Printed in the USA

10 9 8 7 6 5 4 3 2 1

Contents

Introduction

Circular designs are balanced and calm. Stars are exciting.

Put the two together and you have a balanced *and* exciting quilt!

I recommend that you read all the instructions before you begin. If some of the techniques are new to you, you will love the bonus videos that I made to go with each block and more (see page 79).

Sizzle was the 2019 Block of the Month for TheQuiltShow.com. As part of that program, my friend Barbara Black wrote a blog post to go with each block that you may find helpful. Go to her blog (bbquiltmaker.blogspot.com) and enter "Sizzle" in the search field.

I hope you enjoy making your very own Sizzle quilt!

Sizzle Quilt #1, cool colorway, by Becky Goldsmith

Getting Started

ABOUT THE QUILT

Nine foundation paper-pieced blocks combine with machine-appliquéd borders to create a sizzling quilt that is loads of fun to sew!

FINISHED QUILT: 70″ × 70″ • FINISHED BLOCK: 20″ × 20″

FINISHED SIDE BORDERS: 5″ × 60″ • FINISHED TOP/BOTTOM BORDERS: 5″ × 70″

Be sure to follow the yardage requirements for your chosen colorway! The color placement varies a bit between the quilts and your fabric amounts per color will vary accordingly.

Sizzle Quilt #2, warm colorway, by Becky Goldsmith

FABRIC REQUIREMENTS

About the Fabric Requirements

Fabric requirements are based on a 40″ width and include a little extra
for shrinkage from prewashing and for cutting mistakes.

Set aside any leftover fabric from the blocks, borders, and block corners.
You may be able to use these small pieces as you work through the quilt.

Fabric Preparation

Prewash your fabric to remove excess dye, finishes, and to shrink the fabric. Wash in the washer, and dry in the dryer. Fold the fabric when it is warm from the dryer. Iron the fabric with steam when you are ready to use it.

Fabrics: Cool colorway	SKU/Color	Blocks	Yardage
	White	9 blocks, block corners, borders	4 yards
	Cream	Block corners	¾ yard
	Light gray	Block corners	1¼ yards
	Honey gold	Borders	⅛ yard
	Cornflower blue	2, 3, 4, 5, 7, 9	⅞ yard
	Medium blue	1, 2, 5	½ yard
	Dark periwinkle	1, 5, 7, 8, borders	¾ yard
	Periwinkle	3, 7	⅜ yard
	Light aqua	1, 4, 5, 6, 7, 8, 9, borders, binding	2 yards
	Aqua	1, 2, 3, 4, 5, 7	⅞ yard
	Gray aqua	7	¼ yard
	Dark aqua	6, borders	⅞ yard
	Teal	4, 8, 9, borders	1 yard
	Yellow-green	5, 7, 8, 9	⅜ yard
	Chartreuse	1, 2, 3, 4, 6, 9	⅞ yard
	Fern	2, 6, 8, borders	¾ yard
	Lime	5, 6, 9	½ yard
	Grass	4, 7, borders	½ yard
Fabric for backing and sleeve			5 yards

Fabrics: Warm colorway	SKU/Color	Blocks	Yardage
	Canary	1, 2, 3, 4, 5, 6, 7, 8, 9	1 yard
	Sunflower	Block corners, 4	½ yard
	Peach	2, 3, 4, 5, 8, 9, top/bottom borders	1 yard
	Tiger	1, 3, 6, 9	⅔ yard
	Marmalade	1, 6	½ yard
	Pine	1	¼ yard
	Grass	Outer borders	⅓ yard
	Shamrock	4, 9	⅓ yard
	Fern	2, 4, 5, 8	⅔ yard
	Lime	4, 6, 7, 9, top/bottom borders	⅞ yard
	Beetle green	6, 7	⅓ yard
	Pear	Side border	¼ yard
	Carrot	9; Block corners: 1, 2, 3, 4, 5, 6, 7, 9	¾ yard
	Tarte	3, 4, 5	⅔ yard
	Poppy	7, 8, side borders	1⅛ yards
	Tomato	Block corners: 1, 2, 3, 4, 5, 6, 7, 9; top/bottom borders	1½ yards
	Barn	3, 6, 7, top/bottom borders	¾ yard
	Pomegranate	8	¼ yard
	Cosmos	2	⅛ yard
	Sangria	2	¼ yard
	Dahlia	1	⅛ yard
	Beetle blue	Circles in borders	⅛ yard
	Iris	Blocks, borders, binding	4½ yards
Fabric for backing and sleeve			5¼ yards

NOTIONS

- **Simple Foundations Translucent Vellum Paper*:**
  3 packages of 30 sheets (You will use 71 sheets.)

- **Essential Self-Adhesive Laminating Sheets*:**
  2 sheets (Sold in packages of 10 sheets.)

- **Clear upholstery vinyl:** 1 yard

- **Sharpie Ultra Fine Point Permanent Marker**

* by C&T Publishing

For turned-edge machine appliqué:

- **Quilter's Freezer Paper Sheets*:**
  2 packages of 10 sheets

- **Quilters Select Glue Stick with Refills**

- **Wood cuticle stick with 2 flat ends:** 1 or more

- **Sandpaper board:** Or use a sheet
  of fine-grain sandpaper.

- **Batting:** 78″ × 78″

FOUNDATION PAPERS AND TEMPLATES

To ensure success, I encourage you to follow the foundation paper-piecing directions provided, even if you have used a different method in the past.

Prepare the Foundation Papers

Foundation paper piecing is faster and more precise when you can see through the paper, which is why I use Simple Foundations Translucent Vellum Paper (by C&T Publishing).

1. Make the required number of copies for each block on vellum. To save time, you can download and print the blocks directly onto your vellum. For the block patterns, you can use the printed patterns for Blocks 1–9 (pages 56–67) or download them at:

tinyurl.com/11416-patterns-download

2. Cut the foundation paper-piecing patterns down the center of the outer dashed lines.
IMPORTANT: *Do not leave excess paper around your foundation papers.*

3. Keep the foundation papers for each block together with clips or in plastic bags.

Make the Block Corner Template

1. Using laminate or template plastic, make the block corner template. *Note:* The pattern needs to be taped together before making the template.

2. Cut the template out down the center of the outer dashed line.

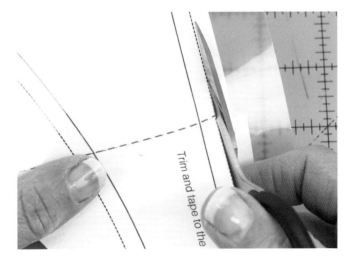

SEWING AND CONSTRUCTION

Seam Allowances

All machine piecing is designed for ¼˝ seam allowances.

Foundation Paper-Piecing Tips

- *Always sew on the solid line*, with the printed side of the paper up, facing you, and the fabric next to the feed dogs.

- If the solid seamline goes to the edges of paper, sew to the edge of the paper.

- If the solid line stops at a circle, sew to the end of that line (inside the circle) and backstitch.

- The paper prevents the top and bobbin threads from pulling together tightly. A shorter stitch results in stitches that are less easily pulled apart when you remove the paper.

- Clean away the paper debris and oil the bobbin area every time you change your bobbin. Your machine will be happier.

Sewing on Foundation Paper

1. Place the 1 and 2 fabrics right sides together, matching one raw edge of each.

2. Place the fabric pair, centered, under the vellum. Be sure that the *wrong side* of the first piece of fabric is centered under section 1 on the paper. Line up the edges of the fabric with the *dashed line*.

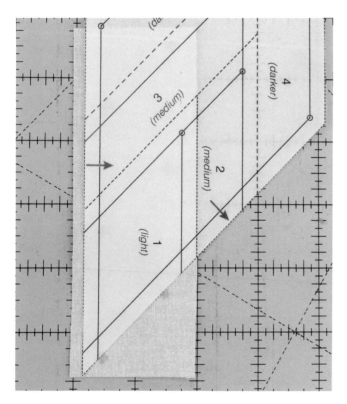

3. Sew on the *solid line* between sections 1 and 2 with the paper right side up. When the end of a seamline is marked with a circle, stop at the end of the line and backstitch.

Sometimes it is easier to begin by backstitching to the circle and then sewing forward to the edge of the block.

4. Press open with an iron or a wooden seam press. Be careful not to stretch the fabric.

5. Fold the paper on the *solid* seamline between sections 1/2 and 3 and use a rotary or Add-A-Quarter ruler and rotary cutter to cut a ¼˝ seam allowance.

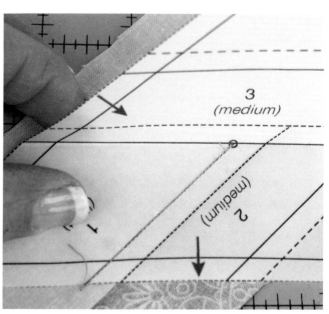

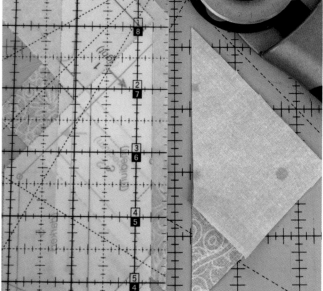

6. Place strip 3 *right sides together* with the raw edge at the far side of 2. Be sure that, when sewn and pressed open, the new strip completely covers the 3 space on the paper.

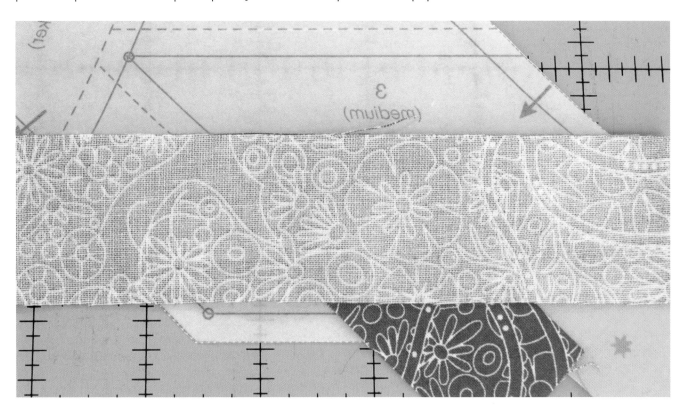

7. Sew strip 3 in place, press, and trim as before. Continue adding strips in order until the paper is covered. Cover one foundation paper completely to be sure your fabric placement is correct, then chain piece the remaining papers.

8. Line up the ¼˝ marks on the ruler with the solid seamline and trim away any fabric that sticks out beyond the edge of the paper.

9. Remove the paper only when indicated in the instructions for each block.

When "1" Is in the Center of the Paper

1. Place the 1 and 2 fabrics right sides together, matching one raw edge of each.

2. Place the fabric pair under 1 on the vellum. Line up the edges of the fabric with the *dashed line* on the 2 side of 1. Be sure that the *wrong side* of the first piece of fabric is centered under 1 on the paper.

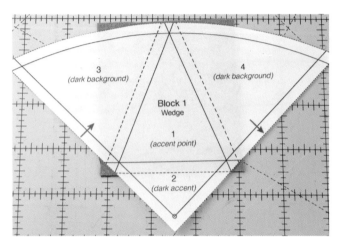

3. Sew on the *solid line* with the paper right side up. Press open.

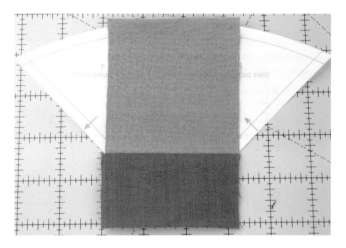

4. Fold the paper back and cut away the excess fabric carefully with a rotary cutter or scissors.

5. Place fabric strip 3 in position and sew it in place. Press open.

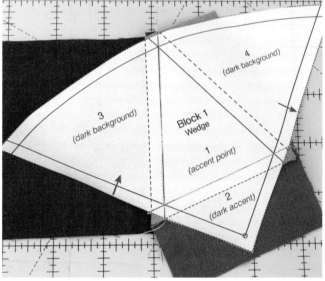

6. On the other side of strip 1, fold the paper back and cut away the excess fabric carefully with a rotary cutter or scissors.

8. Trim away excess fabric.

9. Remove the paper only when indicated.

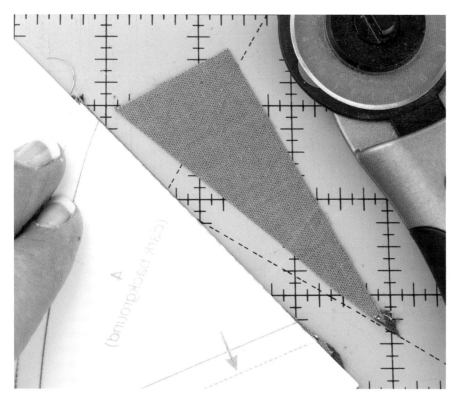

7. Continue adding strips as needed.

TIP: KEEP PIECES FROM SHIFTING

Use a bit of fabric glue to help hold fabrics that are moving in place under the paper. Add the glue to the paper, not the fabric.

Using Positioning Pins

Use positioning pins to accurately match seam inter-sections and points.

1. Sew fabric to the paper pieces.

2. Place sewn pieces right sides together. Push a long pin straight through the matching points of both pieces. Keep the pin vertical *and* perpendicular to the pieces.

3. Pin the pieces together on each side of the positioning pin.

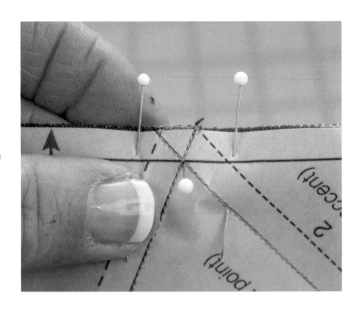

TIP: REMOVE PAPER FROM SEAM ALLOWANCES

After you sew pieced sections together, always remove the paper from the ¼˝ seam allowances.

1. If stitches cross the paper inside the ¼˝ seam allowance, pop the paper free or tear it along the perforations.

2. Crease the paper along the stitched seam, and then tear the paper seam allowance free. Turn the pair over and repeat.

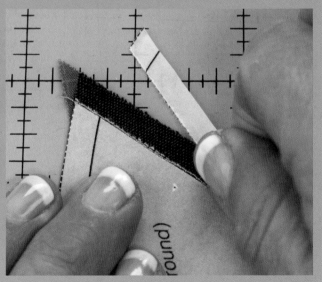

3. Use tweezers to remove stray bits of paper from hard-to-reach areas. I use Apliquick Ergonomic Tweezers.

Remove Paper from Shapes

1. Gently remove paper when indicated in the instructions. Do not pop, pull, or stretch the fabric out of shape. Fold paper at the seamline and gently tear it away in sections.

2. Use an Apliquick Rod, a ballpoint awl, or some other tool to loosen paper from the seams, and use tweezers to remove bits of paper from stubborn areas.

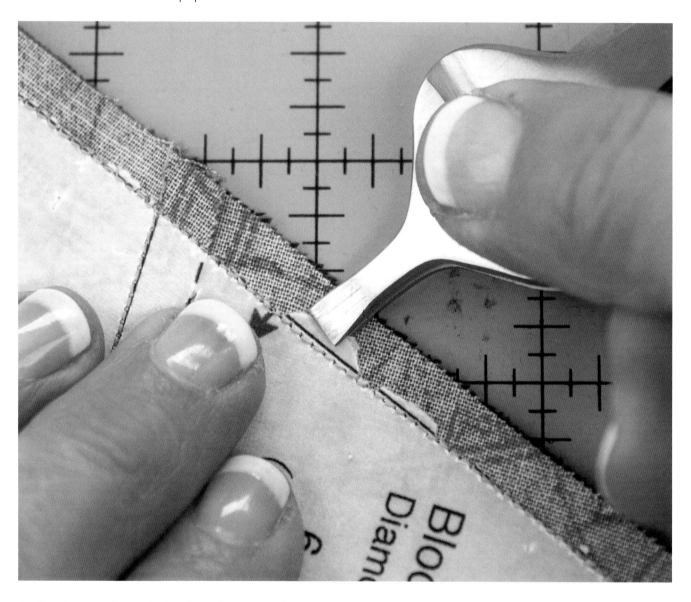

3. Gently press from the back, with steam, after you remove the paper.

Pressing Seam Allowances

1. Press the seam allowances in the direction indicated by the arrows on the paper pieces.

2. If there isn't an arrow to indicate the direction, press the seam allowances in the direction where they lie the flattest. Press from the back, and then the front.

Construct Round Diamond Blocks

Diamond Blocks 1, 2, 3, 5, 6, and 9 are set together as follows.

1. Sew the left side of a Wedge to the top right side of a Diamond, backstitching at the end of a circled seamline.

TIP

Sometimes Wonder Clips hold the Sections together better than pins.

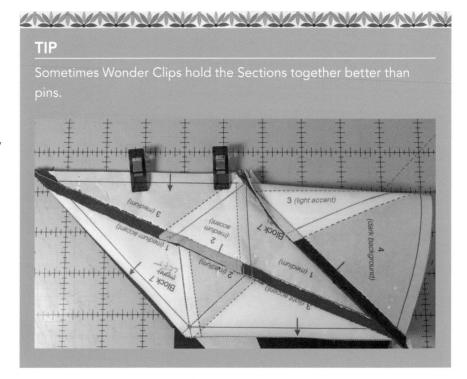

2. Trim away dog-ears as they occur.

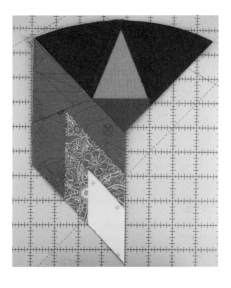

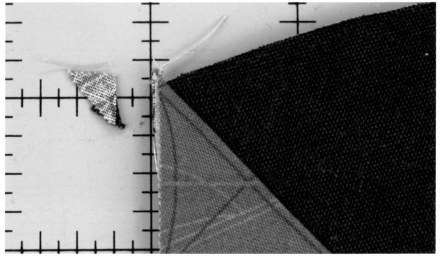

3. Remove the paper from the seam allowances.

4. Press the seam allowances in the direction of the arrows.

5. Pin the seam allowance at the bottom of the wedge out of the way as necessary.

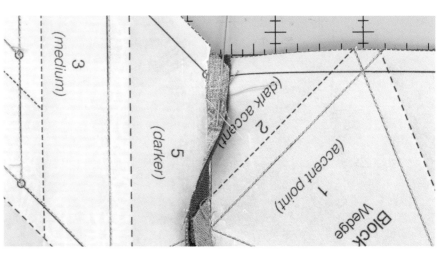

6. Pin the bottom of 2 Diamond/Wedge units together, using positioning pins to match points. Ignore the Wedges for now.

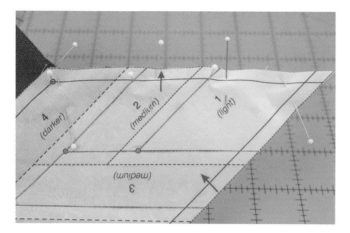

7. Sew the Diamonds together, backstitching at the end of the circled seamline.

8. Remove the pin holding the seam allowances out of the way. Carefully bring together the top left edge of the Diamond with the right edge of the Wedge. Use positioning pins to match the points and pin the shapes together.

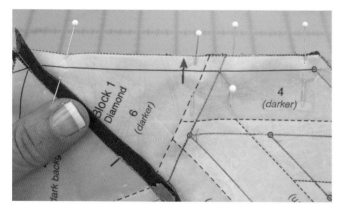

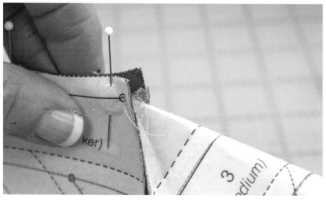

Crease the Diamond at the base of the wedge as needed.

9. Sew slowly and carefully. Backstitch at the circle.

10. Remove the paper from the seam allowances.

11. Press the seam allowances in the direction of the arrows.

12. Repeat Steps 4–9 to make a total of 4 Diamond/Wedge pairs. Sew together, creating 2 halves of the block.

13. Use positioning pins to match the center and points of the Diamonds. Pin the halves of the block together; ignore the Wedges.

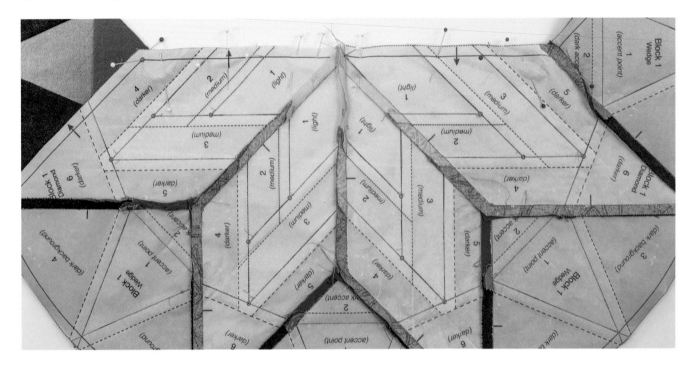

14. Sew the 2 halves of the blocks together at the Diamonds only. Backstitch at circled points.

15. Refer to Step 6 and sew the Wedges and adjacent Diamonds together.

16. Remove the paper from the seam allowances. Press the seam allowances in the direction indicated by the arrows.

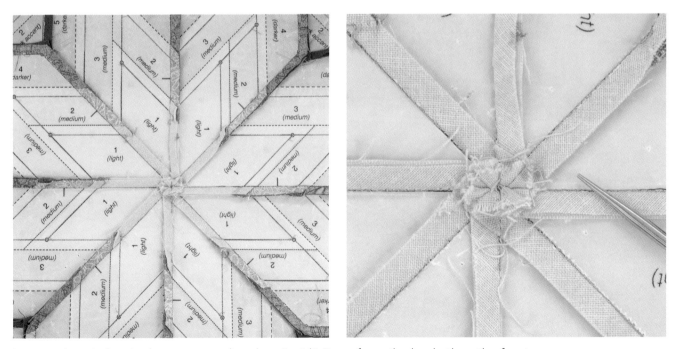

Loosen the stitches in the center so that they "twirl" Press from the back, then the front.

17. Carefully remove the paper from the round block. Do not stretch or pull the block, be gentle.
Use tweezers to remove bits of paper where necessary.

Construct Centers for Blocks 4, 8, and 9

You will use the black dots on the curved seamlines in Block 8 only.

1. Sew the fabric to 2 Center paper pieces.

2. Pin the Centers together, using a positioning pin and additional pins.

3. Sew the Centers together on the solid line.

4. Refer to Tip: Remove Paper from Seam Allowances (page 14) and remove the paper in the seam allowances.

5. Press the seam allowances in the direction indicated by the arrows. Loosen the stitches at the center and "twirl" the seam allowances. Press from the back.

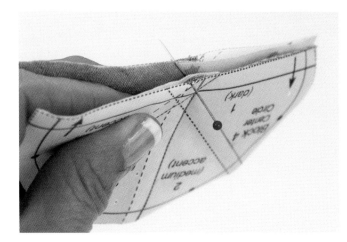

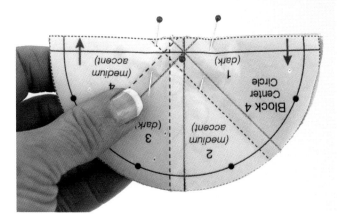

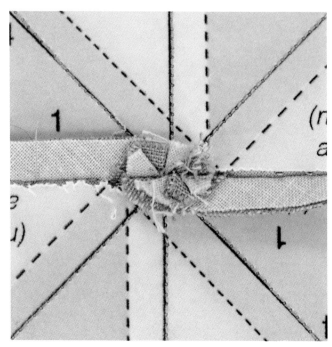

Construct Ring Sections for Blocks 4, 8, and 9

1. Make the copies of the Block foundation paper pattern on vellum and cut out the foundation paper pieces on the outer dashed lines.

2. Sew the fabric to the paper pieces in sequence. Position each fabric strip so that it will cover the next space on the paper.

3. The edges of the Sections are not straight. Change the placement of the ruler to match each straight seamline as you trim away the excess fabric around each Section.

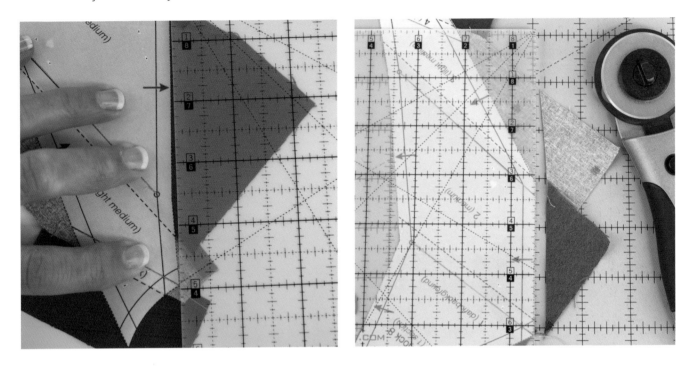

Cut the curved edges slowly and carefully with a rotary cutter or scissors.

Construct Rings for Blocks 4, 8, and 9

Use a bit of fabric glue to help hold the fabric in place on the paper as needed.

1. Tear the paper in the seam allowance at each circled inner point. Repeat for all inner points.

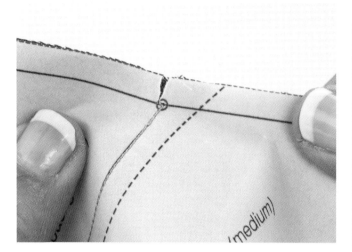

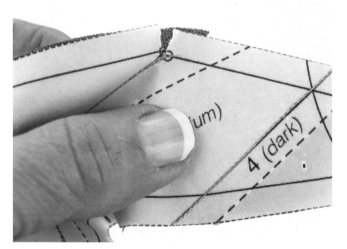

2. Place 2 Sections right sides together with the circled, inner points on top, facing you.

3. Work from the outside of the Ring, toward the center of the Ring, one straight seam at a time. Use positioning pins to match points.

4. Sew from the outside edge of the Ring Sections to the circled end of the seamline, and backstitch. Remove the Sections from your sewing machine.

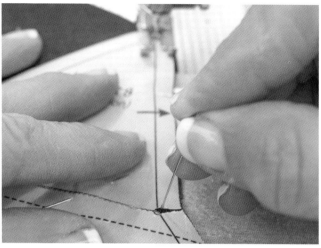

5. Use a positioning pin to match the points at the end of the next straight seamline.

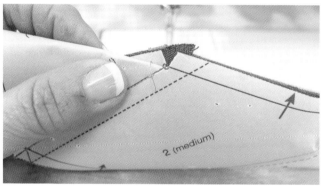

Fold and crease the paper and fabric at the end of your last stitched line so that the pieces lie flat against the bed of the machine when you sew. Pin as needed to keep the raw edges together.

6. Sew from the end of the previous seam to the next circled point, backstitching at each end.

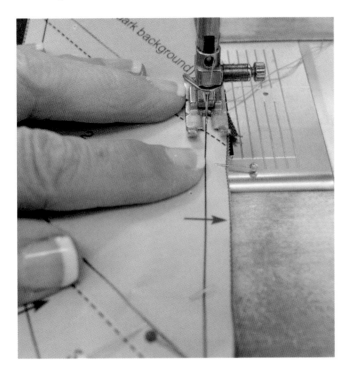

7. Continue in this manner until the 2 Sections have been sewn together.

8. Remove the paper from the seam allowances.

9. Press the seam allowances in the direction of the arrows.

10. In the same manner, sew the remaining Sections together into pairs. Sew pairs together into fours. Sew fours together to make half-blocks.

11. Sew the half-blocks together to make a ring with a hole in the center.

12. Use a rotary cutter or scissors and trim away the dog-ears at the center of the Ring.

13. Gently remove the paper from the Ring.

14. Sew the Ring into the appropriate Block Corners. This will protect the outer bias edges of the Ring when you set in the Center Circle.

Prepare the Block Corners

1. Cut corner rectangles as directed for each block.

2. Place the fabric rectangle right side up on a sandpaper board. The sandpaper keeps the fabric from shifting as you trace around the template.

Place the Corner Template in a corner, right side up, on top of a fabric rectangle.

3. Trace around the short and curved edges of the template. Repeat for the opposite corner of the rectangle.

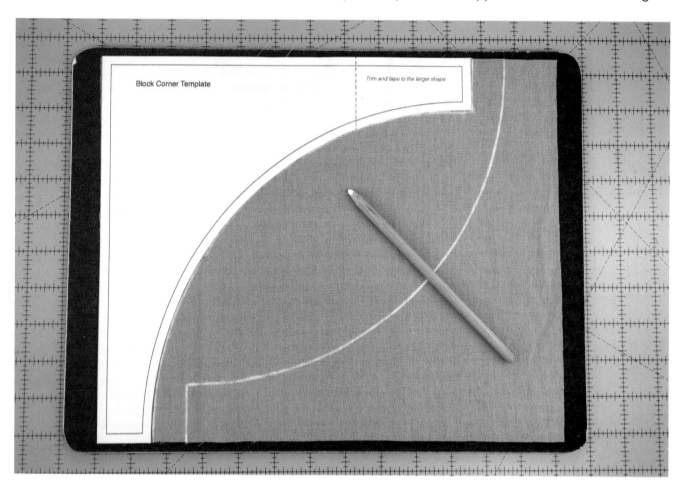

4. Cut out the block corners along the inside edge of the drawn lines with scissors.

5. Sew the corners right sides together along the short sides to make a square with a hole in the center. Press the seam allowances in one direction.

SET-IN CIRCLES
Setting Round Blocks into the Block Corners

These shapes look like they won't fit together, but they do. It's like magic!

The round blocks have top, bottom, right, left, and diagonal centers. These centers fall on points, which makes matching and pinning easier.

Note: Watch Your Color Placement
Always refer to the photo of the block you are working on. Choose the correct Corner colors and be sure they are arranged correctly.

1. Remove the paper from the round blocks. Press gently from the back, and then from the front. I use steam.

2. Fold each corner fabric between the seams to find the diagonal centers. Mark the diagonal centers with a pin.

3. Place the Block Corners on top of a round block with right sides up. Align the Corner seams with the top, bottom, left, and right center points of the Round Block.

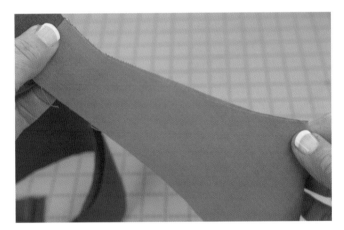

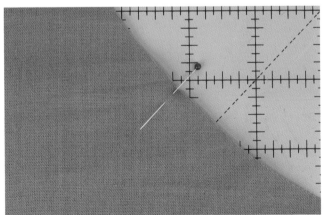

4. Carefully fold the Corners at the seams, over the round block, bringing the raw edges together. Use positioning pins to match the seams with the points. Pin the top, bottom, left, and right center points in place.

5. Match and pin the diagonal center points in place in the same manner.

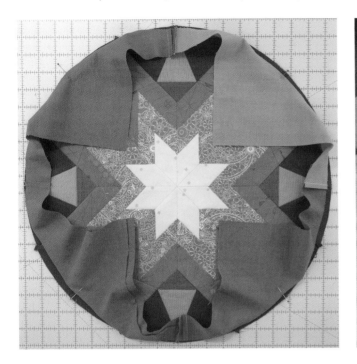 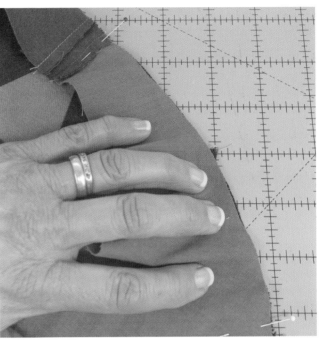

6. Gently work the raw edges together between the pinned center points. Use positioning pins and as many pins as you need to hold the edges together smoothly.

7. Place the round block flat on the bed of your sewing machine. *Always* sew with the concave curve, the Corners, on top.

8. Watch your ¼˝ seam allowance as you slowly sew around the circle. Don't try to pull the fabric straight in front of the presser foot. Let it flow into place, following the circular edge.

Use a tool as necessary to hold raw edges even and the seam allowances flat as you sew over them. Do not let seam allowances on the underside of the block flip out of position.

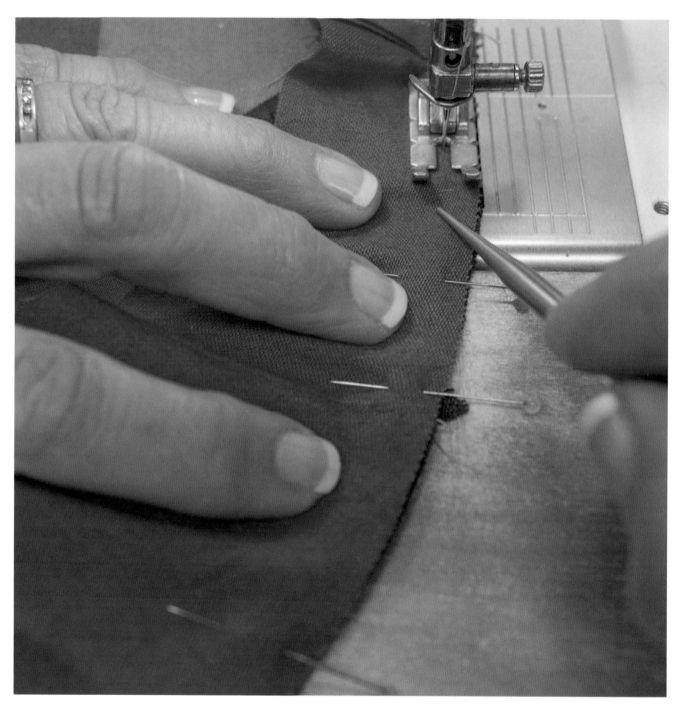

9. Press the seam allowances away from the center, toward the Corners.

Setting Center Circles into Blocks 4, 7, and 8

The Center circle is handled in the same way as is described in Setting Round Blocks into the Block Corners (page 24); however, the Center is smaller. Take your time, think calm thoughts, and you will be just fine.

Note: Take Your Time on Block 8
In Block 8 (page 46), the *seams* of the Center Circle fall between Ring points. The dots on the Center Circle papers are used only in this block. In Blocks 4 and 7, the seamlines are aligned with Ring points.

1. On the Center Circle, mark the north, south, east, west, and diagonal centers with pins.

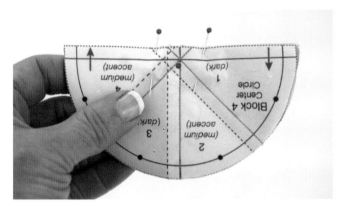

2. Place the Ring over the Center Circle. Be sure that the colors in the Circle are oriented correctly.

3. Carefully fold the Ring over the round block, bringing the raw edges together, matching the points marked with pins. Pin. Use as many pins as needed to hold the raw edges together around the Circle.

TIP: FOLD AND PIN

After just a few pins, you will need to pick the Center and Ring up to pin.

4. Place the Center flat on the bed of your sewing machine. Always sew with the Ring on top.

5. Watch your ¼″ seam allowance as you slowly sew around the circle. Let the fabric flow into place, following the circular edge. Gently rearrange the block as you sew to keep it from bunching up.

Use a tool, such as an Apliquick Rod, to hold raw edges together and to guide the fabric under the presser foot. Do not let seam allowances flip out of position on the underside.

6. Remove the paper from the Center Circle.

7. Press the seam allowances toward the Center of the block.

APPLIQUÉ THE BORDERS

I used turned-edge machine appliqué for the borders of my quilts. You are welcome to use your favorite appliqué method. If you want to print the template pattern onto your favorite appliqué medium, you can use the printed patterns for individual appliqué pieces (pages 71, 77, and 78) or download them at:

tinyurl.com/11416-patterns-download

FINISHED SIDE BORDERS: 5˝ × 60˝ • FINISHED TOP/BOTTOM BORDERS: 5˝ × 70˝

Make Placement Overlays for the Outer Borders

Follow the instructions for the Side Borders (page 50) and Top/Bottom Borders (page 52), and copy, trim, and tape together the pattern pieces to make one 5˝ × 60˝ Side Border pattern and one 5˝ × 70˝ Top/Bottom Border pattern.

1. Cut 2 strips of clear upholstery vinyl (with its tissue paper lining) 5˝ wide. Tape the strips together end to end, and trim to 5˝ × 60˝ for the Side Border.

2. Cut 2 strips of clear upholstery vinyl (with its tissue paper lining) 5˝ wide. Tape the strips together end to end, and trim to 5˝ × 70˝ for the Top/Bottom Border.

3. Tape the Side Border pattern to a table with painter's tape.

4. Place the 5˝ × 60˝ strip of clear vinyl over the pattern.

5. Trace the dashed centerlines, the pattern lines, and the numbers onto the vinyl with a black Sharpie Ultra Fine Point Permanent Marker.

Be sure to mark the center of the overlay.

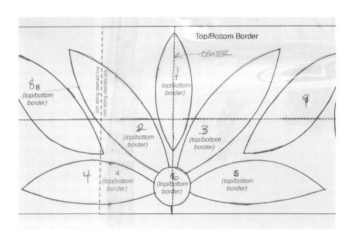

6. Make the placement overlay for the 5˝ × 70˝ Top/Bottom Border in the same manner.

Prepare Machine Appliqué Shapes

1. Copy the template patterns onto freezer paper sheets.

2. Cut them out on the drawn line.

3. Iron the shape onto the right side of the appliqué fabric.

4. Cut out the shape adding a scant ¼˝ seam allowance.

5. Finger-press the seam allowance to the back of the shape at edge of the freezer paper.

6. Use a cuticle stick to apply a little dab of glue to the wrong side of the seam allowance and then stick it in place to the back of the appliqué shape. Repeat to hold the seam allowance under neatly.

Use the Positioning Overlay

1. Press each border background strip in half horizontally and vertically to create a center grid.

2. Place a Side Border background right side up on your ironing board.

3. Place the overlay right side up on top of the background. Line up the pressed-in center grid in your background with the center grid of the overlay. Pin the overlay and background to the ironing board along the top of the border.

4. Place an appliqué shape right side up under the overlay, on top of the background. Match the appliqué piece to the shape drawn on the overlay.

5. Fold the overlay back, remove the freezer paper from the top of the appliqué piece, and carefully pin the appliqué in place.

Slide a rigid piece of paper under the background fabric to make pinning easier.

6. Apply glue to the turned under seam allowances lightly and then position the appliqué in place on the background. You may need to add pins to hold the shapes in place. You don't want them to move out of position when you are sewing at the machine.

7. Remove the vinyl overlay before stitching your appliqué in place.

Special notes:

• Place appliqué pieces onto the background in numerical order.

• Be sure that the overlay does not scoot out of position as you use it.

• On smaller shapes, apply glue lightly to the seam allowances before you place them on the background. Move quickly so that the glue doesn't dry out.

Sew the Appliqué in Place

1. Refer to Use the Positioning Overlay (previous page) and pin or glue appliqué shapes to the border background.

2. Load your sewing machine with fine thread in a color that matches the first appliqué piece.

3. Place an open-toe embroidery foot on your machine.

4. Place the border under the needle 1–3 stitches in front of where you want to begin sewing. Bring the bobbin thread to the top. Backstitch, and then sew forward.

5. Sew very close to the prepared edge of the appliqué shape with either a straight or blanket stitch. Straight stitches will blend in with your machine quilting stitches; blanket stitches are a little more visible.

Sew slowly. Use a tool in front of the needle to hold and control the fabric. Remember that you are the boss—take control of the fabric as you guide it under the needle.

6. Continue in this manner until the appliqué shapes are sewn to the border.

7. When the appliqué is complete, press the borders from the back. Refer to the patterns for trimming instructions.

Constructing the Blocks and Borders

Note: The block instructions are presented in order of block difficulty, *not* according to block placement in quilts. For the different block placements in the cool and warm colorways, see the quilt assembly diagrams (page 54).

BLOCK 1
FINISHED BLOCK: 20″ × 20″

Construct the Block

1. Make 8 copies of the Block 1 foundation paper pattern on vellum.

2. Refer to the Sewing and Appliqué (page 9) to make the Diamonds and Wedges and set them together.

3. Sew together 1 cream and 3 light gray Block Corners. Sew the round block into the Block Corners.

4. Gently press the block from the back, and then from the front. Set this block aside until you are ready to finish the quilt.

Fabric Cutting: Cool Colorway   *WOF = width of fabric*

DIAMOND

#	Color	Strips	Individual pieces
1	Dark periwinkle	2 @ 2″ × WOF	8 @ 2″ × 5½″
2	Aqua	1 @ 1¾″ × WOF	8 @ 1¾″ × 4″
3	Aqua	2 @ 1¾″ × WOF	8 @ 1¾″ × 6″
4 & 5	Medium blue	2 @ 1¾″ × WOF	16 @ 1¾″ × 4½″
6	Medium blue	1 @ 3½″ × WOF	8 @ 3½″ × 4″

WEDGE

#	Color	Strips	Individual pieces
1	Light aqua	1 @ 3¼″ × WOF	8 @ 3¼″ × 3¾″
2	Chartreuse	1 @ 2″ × WOF	8 @ 2″ × 3½″
3 & 4	White	See next chart.	

WHITE

Cut **all** the *white* fabric now and use in **all** the blocks as needed.

White	Strips	Individual pieces
Wedges in round blocks	15 @ 4″ × WOF	144 @ 4″ × 4″ (16 per block)
Outer borders	8 @ 7″ × WOF	

CORNERS

Refer to Prepare the Block Corners (page 23) and cut all the Block Corners. Reserve the Corners that you don't use for Blocks 2–9.

Color	Strips	Individual pieces
White	1 @ 10½″ × WOF	2 @ 10½″ × 13″ (4 corners)
Cream	2 @ 10½″ × WOF	6 @ 10½″ × 13″ (12 corners)
Light gray	4 strips @ 10½″ × WOF	10 @ 10½″ × 13″ (20 corners)

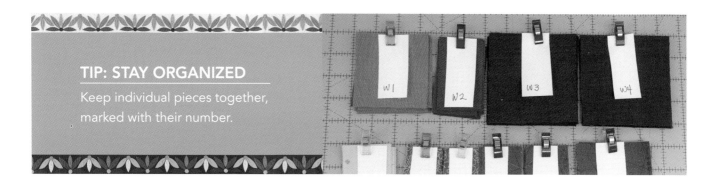

TIP: STAY ORGANIZED
Keep individual pieces together, marked with their number.

Fabric Cutting: Warm Colorway   *WOF = width of fabric*

DIAMOND

#	Color (*value*)	Strips	Individual pieces
1	Canary (*light*)	2 @ 2″ × WOF	8 @ 2″ × 5½″
2	Tiger (*medium*)	1 @ 1¾″ × WOF	8 @ 1¾″ × 4″
3	Tiger (*medium*)	2 @ 1¾″ × WOF	8 @ 1¾″ × 6″
4 & 5	Marmalade (*dark*)	2 @ 1¾″ × WOF	16 @ 1¾″ × 4½″
6	Marmalade (*dark*)	1 @ 3¼″ × WOF	8 @ 3¼″ × 4″

WEDGE

#	Color (*value*)	Strips	Individual pieces
1	Pine (*dark*)	1 @ 3¼″ × WOF	8 @ 3¼″ × 3½″
2	Dahlia (*medium*)	1 @ 2″ × WOF	8 @ 2″ × 3¼″
3 & 4	Iris (*dark*)	See next chart.	

IRIS

Cut **all** the *iris* fabric now and use in **all** the blocks as needed. Reserve the remaining fabric for the binding.

Iris (*dark*)	Strips	Individual pieces
Wedges in round blocks (*dark background*)	15 @ 4″ × WOF	144 @ 4″ × 4″ (16 per block)
Outer borders	8 @ 7″ × WOF	

CORNERS

Refer to Prepare the Block Corners (page 23) and cut all of the Block Corners. Reserve the Corners that you don't use for Blocks 2–9.

Color (*value*)	Strips	Individual pieces
Sunflower (*light*)	1 @ 10½″ × WOF	2 @ 10½″ × 13″ (4 corners)
Carrot (*medium*)	2 @ 10½″ × WOF	6 @ 10½″ × 13″ (12 corners)
Tomato (*dark*)	4 strips @ 10½″ × WOF	10 @ 10½″ × 13″ (20 corners)

BLOCK 2
FINISHED BLOCK: 20″ × 20″

Fabric Cutting: Cool Colorway   *WOF = width of fabric*

SECTION 1

#	Color	Strips	Individual pieces
1	Medium blue	1 @ 2¼″ × WOF	8 @ 2¼″ × 4½″
2	Fern	1 @ 1¾″ × WOF	8 @ 1¾″ × 3½″
3	Fern	1 @ 3″ × WOF	8 @ 3″ × 3¼″

SECTION 2

#	Color	Strips	Individual pieces
1	Cornflower blue	1 @ 2″ × WOF	8 @ 2″ × 4½″
2	Aqua	1 @ 1¾″ × WOF	8 @ 1¾″ × 3½″
3	Fern	1 @ 1¾″ × WOF	8 @ 1¾″ × 3½″

SECTION 3

#	Color	Strips	Individual pieces
1	Aqua	1 @ 2¼″ × WOF	8 @ 2¼″ × 3½″
2, 3	Fern	2 @ 3″ × WOF	16 @ 3″ × 3″

WEDGE

#	Color	Strips	Individual pieces
1	Chartreuse	1 @ 3″ × WOF	8 @ 3″ × 5″
2, 3	White	From Block 1	16 @ 4″ × 4″

Construct the Block

1. Make 8 copies of the Block 2 foundation paper pattern on vellum.

2. Refer to Sewing and Appliqué (page 9) to make the Diamonds and Wedges and set them together.

Fabric Cutting: Warm Colorway   *WOF = width of fabric*

SECTION 1

#	Color (*value*)	Strips	Individual pieces
1	Peach (*light*)	1 @ 2¼″ × WOF	8 @ 2¼″ × 4¾″
2	Fern (*medium*)	1 @ 2″ × WOF	8 @ 2″ × 3½″
3	Fern (*medium*)	1 @ 3″ × WOF	8 @ 3″ × 3″

SECTION 2

#	Color (*value*)	Strips	Individual pieces
1	Cosmos (*medium*)	1 @ 2″ × WOF	8 @ 2″ × 4½″
2	Sangria (*dark*)	1 @ 2″ × WOF	8 @ 2″ × 3½″
3	Fern (*medium*)	1 @ 2″ × WOF	8 @ 2″ × 3½″

SECTION 3

#	Color (*value*)	Strips	Individual pieces
1	Sangria (*dark*)	1 @ 2¼″ × WOF	8 @ 2¼″ × 3½″
2, 3	Fern (*medium*)	2 @ 3″ × WOF	16 @ 3″ × 3″

WEDGE

#	Color (*value*)	Strips	Individual pieces
1	Canary (*light*)	1 @ 3″ × WOF	8 @ 3″ × 5″
2, 3	Iris (*dark*)	From Block 1	16 @ 4″ × 4″

Special note:

Match the sides of Section 1 and Section 2 that are marked with stars. Use positioning pins as needed to match points. Pin, and then sew the sections together.

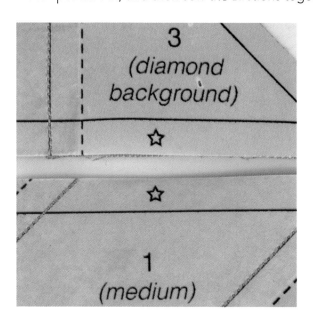

3. Sew together 2 cream and 2 light gray Block Corners. Sew the round block into the Block Corners.

4. Gently press the block from the back, and then from the front. Set this block aside until you are ready to finish the quilt.

BLOCK 3

FINISHED BLOCK: 20˝ × 20˝

Fabric Cutting: Cool Colorway

WOF = width of fabric

DIAMOND

#	Color	Strips	Individual pieces
1	Periwinkle	3 @ 1¼˝ × WOF	8 @ 1¼˝ × 11˝
2, 3	Cornflower blue	4 @ 1¼˝ × WOF	16 @ 1¼˝ × 10˝
4, 5	Aqua	4 @ 1¼˝ × WOF	16 @ 1¼˝ × 8˝
6, 7	Chartreuse	3 @ 1¼˝ × WOF	16 @ 1¼˝ × 6˝

WEDGE

#	Color	Strips	Individual pieces
1	Periwinkle	2 @ 1¼˝ × WOF	8 @ 1¼˝ × 5½˝
2, 3	Cornflower blue	2 @ 1¼˝ × WOF	16 @ 1¼˝ × 5˝
4, 5	Aqua	2 @ 1¼˝ × WOF	16 @ 1¼˝ × 4˝
6, 7	White	From Block 1	16 @ 4˝ × 4˝

Construct the Block

The instructional photos show the warm colorway.

1. Make 8 copies of the Block 3 foundation paper pattern on vellum.

2. Refer to Sewing and Appliqué (page 9) to make the Diamonds and Wedges and set them together.

Fabric Cutting: Warm Colorway *WOF = width of fabric*

DIAMOND

#	Color (*value*)	Strips	Individual pieces
1	Barn (*dark*)	3 @ 1¼″ × WOF	8 @ 1¼″ × 11″
2, 3	Tarte (*medium*)	4 @ 1¼″ × WOF	16 @ 1¼″ × 10″
4, 5	Tiger (*medium*)	4 @ 1¼″ × WOF	16 @ 1¼″ × 8″
6, 7	Canary (*light*)	3 @ 1¼″ × WOF	16 @ 1¼″ × 6″

WEDGE

#	Color (*value*)	Strips	Individual pieces
1	Barn (*dark*)	2 @ 1½″ × WOF	8 @ 1½″ × 5½″
2, 3	Tarte (*medium*)	2 @ 1″ × WOF	16 @ 1″ × 5″
4, 5	Peach (*light*)	2 @ 1½″ × WOF	16 @ 1½″ × 4″
6, 7	Iris (*dark*)	From Block 1	16 @ 4″ × 4″

Special notes:

• Be sure to center the strips as you add them to the Diamonds. Trim away the excess fabric.

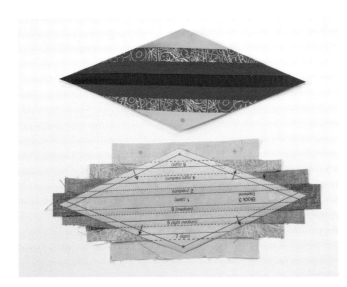

• The inside point is marked on the Diamond papers. If you accidentally turn the Diamonds around, the arrows will point the wrong way. If that happens to you, just press the seam allowances in the same direction, around the block.

• Pin the Diamond/Wedge seam allowance out of the way as you construct the round block.

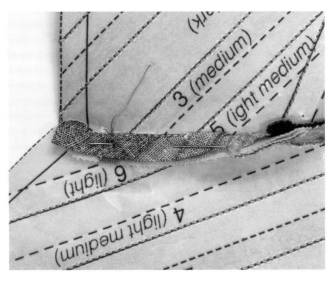

3. Choose 1 cream and 3 light gray Block Corners and sew the round block into the Block Corners.

4. Gently press the block from the back, and then from the front. Set this block aside until you are ready to finish the quilt.

BLOCK 4

FINISHED BLOCK: 20″ × 20″

Fabric Cutting: Cool Colorway   *WOF = width of fabric*

CENTER

#	Color	Strips	Individual pieces
1 & 3	Teal	1 @ 2¼″ × WOF	4 @ 2¼″ × 3¼″
2 & 4	Grass	1 @ 2¼″ × WOF	4 @ 2¼″ × 2¼″

DIAMOND

#	Color *(value)*	Strips	Individual pieces
1	Light aqua	2 @ 2¾″ × WOF	8 @ 2¾″ × 8½″
2 & 3	Chartreuse	4 @ 1¾″ × WOF	16 @ 1¾″ × 7½″
4	Grass	1 @ 2½″ × WOF	4 @ 2½″ × 4″
4	Teal	1 @ 2½″ × WOF	4 @ 2½″ × 4″

WEDGE

#	Color	Strips	Individual pieces
1	Cornflower blue	2 @ 1¾″ × WOF	8 @ 1¾″ × 5½″
2 & 3	Aqua	2 @ 1¾″ × WOF	16 @ 1¾″ × 5″
4 & 5	White	From Block 1	16 @ 4″ × 4″

Construct the Block

The instructional photos show the warm colorway.

1. Make 8 copies of the Block 4 foundation paper pattern on vellum.

Set aside the extra Center Circle papers to use in Blocks 8 and 9.

2. Refer to Sewing and Appliqué (page 9) to make the Center Circle, the Diamonds, and Wedges.

Special notes:

- There are 4 Diamond Sections with teal triangles and 4 with grass triangles.

- Sew 1 teal and 1 grass Diamond/Wedge unit together. Do not switch the positions of the teal and grass triangles as you sew them together into pairs.

- Be sure to pin the seam allowance out of the way when you sew the Wedge to the adjacent Diamond.

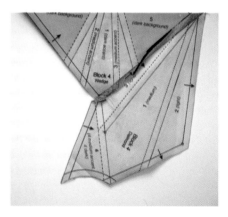

Fabric Cutting: Warm Colorway   *WOF = width of fabric*

CENTER

#	Color (*value*)	Strips	Individual pieces
1 & 3	Tarte (*dark*)	1 @ 2¼˝ × WOF	4 @ 2¼˝ × 3˝
2 & 4	Lime (*light*)	1 @ 2¼˝ × WOF	4 @ 2¼˝ × 3˝

DIAMOND

#	Color (*value*)	Strips	Individual pieces
1	Peach (*light*)	2 @ 2¾˝ × WOF	8 @ 2¾˝ × 8½˝
2 & 3	Canary (*light*)	4 @ 1¾˝ × WOF	16 @ 1¾˝ × 7½˝
4	Lime (*light*)	1 @ 2½˝ × WOF	4 @ 2½˝ × 4˝
4	Tarte (*dark*)	1 @ 2½˝ × WOF	4 @ 2½˝ × 4˝

WEDGE

#	Color (*value*)	Strips	Individual pieces
1	Shamrock (*dark*)	2 @ 1¾˝ × WOF	8 @ 1¾˝ × 5½˝
2 & 3	Fern (*medium*)	2 @ 1½˝ × WOF	16 @ 1½˝ × 5˝
4 & 5	Iris (*dark*)	From Block 1	16 @ 4˝ × 4˝

- Fold the Wedge as needed to bring the bottom edges of the Diamond together.

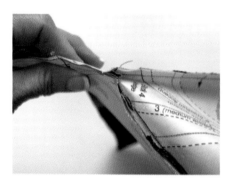

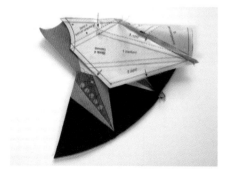

- Press the seam allowances in the direction of the arrows.

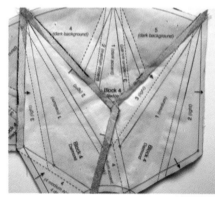

- Sew pairs together into fours, and so on, until the Ring is complete. Then remove the paper from the ring. Trim the dog-ears.

3. Sew together 2 cream and 2 light gray Block Corners. Sew the round block into the Block Corners. Refer to the photo of the block and *be sure* to point the center green star up, toward "north."

4. Set the Center Circle into the center of the block. *Be sure* to place the teal and grass wedges in the Center Circle next to the teal and grass triangle in the Ring.

5. Gently press the block from the back, and then from the front. Set this block aside until you are ready to finish the quilt.

BLOCK 5

FINISHED BLOCK: 20″ × 20″

Fabric Cutting: Cool Colorway   *WOF = width of fabric*

DIAMOND

The Top and Bottom are cut together.

#	Color	Strips	Individual pieces
1	Dark periwinkle	3 @ 1½″ × WOF	16 @ 1½″ × 6½″
2	Medium blue	3 @ 1¼″ × WOF	16 @ 1¼″ × 5¼″
3	Cornflower blue	2 @ 1¼″ × WOF	16 @ 1¼″ × 4½″
4	Light aqua	2 @ 1¼″ × WOF	16 @ 1¼″ × 3½″
5	Aqua	1 @ 1¼″ × WOF	16 @ 1¼″ × 2½″

WEDGE

#	Color	Strips	Individual pieces
1	Lime	1 @ 2″ × WOF	8 @ 2″ × 5″
2	Yellow-green	1 @ 2″ × WOF	8 @ 2″ × 5″
3, 4	White	From Block 1	16 @ 4″ × 4″

Construct the Block

The instructional photos show the warm colorway.

1. Make 8 copies of the Block 5 foundation paper pattern on vellum.

2. Refer to Sewing and Appliqué (page 9) to make the Center Circle, the Diamonds, and Wedges and set them together.

Special notes:

• The strips are narrow—you won't be trimming much away.

• The Top and Bottom Diamonds are mirror images of each other.

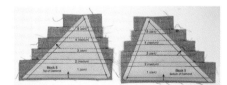

• Sew the Top and Bottom together, using positioning pins as needed. Remove the paper from the paper from the seam allowances.

• Press 4 of the seam allowances toward the Top and 4 to the Bottom.

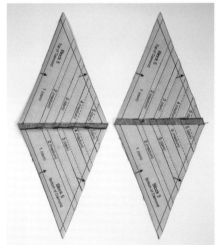

Fabric Cutting: Warm Colorway *WOF = width of fabric*

DIAMOND

The Top and Bottom are cut together.

#	Color (*value*)	Strips	Individual pieces
1, 3, 5	Tarte (*dark*)	6 @ 1¼″ × WOF	16 @ 1¼″ × 6″
			16 @ 1¼″ × 4½″
			16 @ 1¼″ × 2½″
2, 4	Peach (*light*)	4 @ 1¼″ × WOF	16 @ 1¼″ × 5¼″
			16 @ 1¼″ × 3½″

WEDGE

#	Color (*value*)	Strips	Individual pieces
1	Fern (*medium*)	1 @ 2″ × WOF	8 @ 2″ × 5″
2	Canary (*light*)	1 @ 2″ × WOF	8 @ 2″ × 5″
3, 4	Iris (*dark*)	From Block 1	16 @ 4″ × 4″

- Pin the center seam allowances out of the way when you sew the Wedges to the Diamonds.

- Press in the direction of the arrows. Press bulky intersections as flat as you can.

3. Sew together 1 cream and 3 light gray Block Corners. Sew the round block into the Block Corners.

4. Gently press the block from the back, and then from the front. Set this block aside until you are ready to finish the quilt.

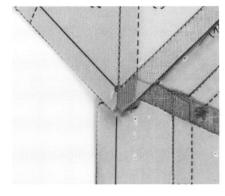

BLOCK 6

FINISHED BLOCK: 20˝ × 20˝

Fabric Cutting: Cool Colorway
WOF = width of fabric

DIAMOND TOP

#	Color	Strips	Individual pieces
1	Dark aqua	3 @ 2¾˝ × WOF	8 @ 2¾˝ × 6˝
2	Chartreuse	2 @ 2¾˝ × WOF	8 @ 2¾˝ × 6˝

Set aside a 2˝ × 2˝ scrap of a dark blue for a 1¼˝ appliquéd center circle.

DIAMOND BOTTOM

#	Color	Strips	Individual pieces
1	Dark aqua	From Diamond Top	8 @ 2½˝ × 6˝
2	Lime	2 @ 2½˝ × WOF	8 @ 2½˝ × 6˝

WEDGE

#	Color	Strips	Individual pieces
1	Fern	1 @ 2˝ × WOF	8 @ 2˝ × 5˝
2	Light aqua	1 @ 2˝ × WOF	8 @ 2˝ × 5˝
3, 4	White	From Block 1	16 @ 4˝ × 4˝

Construct the Block

The instructional photos show the warm colorway.

1. Make 8 copies of the Block 6 foundation paper pattern on vellum.

2. Refer to Sewing and Appliqué (page 9) to make the Center Circle, the Diamonds, and Wedges and set them together.

Special notes:

• Press 4 of the seam allowances toward the Top and 4 to the Bottom.

• Pin the center seam allowances out of the way when you sew the Wedges to the Diamonds.

• Remove the paper at the top and bottom tips of the Diamonds as you sew the block together.

• Cut off dog-ears as they form.

Fabric Cutting: Warm Colorway   *WOF = width of fabric*

DIAMOND TOP

#	Color (*value*)	Strips	Individual pieces
1	Marmalade (*dark*)	2 @ 2½″ × WOF	8 @ 2½″ × 6″
2	Beetle green (*medium*)	2 @ 2½″ × WOF	8 @ 2½″ × 6″

Set aside a 2″ × 2″ scrap of Marmalade for a 1¼″ appliquéd center circle.

DIAMOND BOTTOM

#	Color (*value*)	Strips	Individual pieces
1	Barn (*dark*)	2 @ 2½″ × WOF	8 @ 2½″ × 6″
2	Lime (*medium*)	2 @ 2½″ × WOF	8 @ 2½″ × 6″

WEDGE

#	Color (*value*)	Strips	Individual pieces
1	Tiger (*medium*)	1 @ 2″ × WOF	8 @ 2″ × 5″
2	Canary (*light*)	1 @ 2″ × WOF	8 @ 2″ × 5″
3, 4	Iris (*dark*)	From Block 1	16 @ 4″ × 4″

- There are a lot of seams that come together at the center of the block. It is possible to make the points (mostly) match, but even if you do the center is extremely thick and bulky.

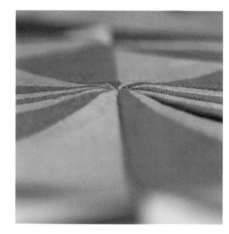

- I decided to appliqué a 1¼″ circle over the bulky center and then trim away the seams from behind. Do this *after* you sew the Corners to the Round Block.

3. Sew together 2 cream and 2 light gray Block Corners. Sew the round block into the Block Corners.

4. Gently press the block from the back, and then from the front. Set this block aside until you are ready to finish the quilt.

BLOCK 7
FINISHED BLOCK: 20˝ × 20˝

Fabric Cutting: Cool Colorway
WOF = width of fabric

DIAMOND: RIGHT SIDE

#	Color	Strips	Individual pieces
1	Dark periwinkle	1 @ 2¼˝ × WOF	8 @ 2¼˝ × 6˝
2	Light aqua	1 @ 3˝ × WOF	8 @ 3˝ × 3˝
3	Cornflower blue	1 @ 2¼˝ × WOF	8 @ 2¼˝ × 6˝

DIAMOND: LEFT SIDE

#	Color	Strips	Individual pieces
1	Gray aqua	1 @ 2¼˝ × WOF	8 @ 2¼˝ × 6˝
2	Periwinkle	1 @ 3˝ × WOF	8 @ 3˝ × 3˝
3	Aqua	1 @ 2¼˝ × WOF	8 @ 2¼˝ × 6˝

WEDGE

#	Color	Strips	Individual pieces
1	Grass	1 @ 2˝ × WOF	8 @ 2˝ × 5˝
2	Yellow-green	1 @ 2˝ × WOF	8 @ 2˝ × 5˝
3, 4	White	From Block 1	16 @ 4˝ × 4˝

Set aside a 2˝ × 2˝ scrap of periwinkle for a 1¼˝ appliquéd center circle.

Construct the Block

The instructional photos show the warm colorway.

1. Make 8 copies of the Block 7 foundation paper pattern on vellum.

2. Refer to Sewing and Appliqué (page 9) to make the Diamonds and Wedges.

Special notes:

• Be sure to place the fabric strips so that they cover the next space after they are pressed open.

• The seams will nest together at the center when you sew the Right and Left sides of the Diamonds together

Fabric Cutting: Warm Colorway   *WOF = width of fabric*

DIAMOND: RIGHT SIDE

#	Color (*value*)	Strips	Individual pieces
1, 3	Poppy (*dark*)	2 @ 4½″ × WOF	16 @ 4½″ × 5″
2	Lime (*medium*)	1 @ 2½″ × WOF	8 @ 2½″ × 3¼″

DIAMOND: LEFT SIDE

#	Color (*value*)	Strips	Individual pieces
1	Lime (*medium*)	1 @ 4½″ × WOF	8 @ 4½″ × 5″
2	Poppy (*dark*)	1 @ 2½″ × WOF	8 @ 2½″ × 3¼″
3	Beetle green (*light*)	1 @ 4½″ × WOF	8 @ 4½″ × 5″

WEDGE

#	Color (*value*)	Strips	Individual pieces
1	Barn (*dark*)	1 @ 2″ × WOF	8 @ 2″ × 5″
2	Canary (*light*)	1 @ 2″ × WOF	8 @ 2″ × 5″
3, 4	Iris (*dark*)	From Block 1	16 @ 4″ × 4″

Set aside a 2″ × 2″ scrap of Barn for a 1¼″ appliquéd center circle.

- Remove the paper at the top and bottom tips of the Diamonds as you sew the block together. Cut away dog-ears as they form.

- There are a lot of seams that come together at the center of the block. To prevent excess bulk at the center, refer to instructions in Block 6 (page 42).

3. Sew together 2 cream and 2 light gray Block Corners and sew the round block into the Block Corners.

4. Gently press the block from the back, and then from the front. Set this block aside until you are ready to finish the quilt.

BLOCK 8

FINISHED BLOCK: 20″ × 20″

Fabric Cutting: Cool Colorway   *WOF = width of fabric*

CENTER

#	Color	Strips	Individual pieces
1, 3	Fern	1 @ 2¼″ × WOF	4 @ 2¼″ × 3¼″
2, 4	Yellow-green	1 @ 2¼″ × WOF	4 @ 2¼″ × 3¼″

RING SECTION

#	Color	Strips	Individual pieces
1	White	From Block 1	16 @ 4″ × 4″
2	Teal	3 @ 3½″ × WOF	16 @ 3½″ × 6¾″
3	Light aqua	3 @ 2″ × WOF	16 @ 2″ × 6″
4	Dark periwinkle	2 @ 1¾″ × WOF	16 @ 1¾″ × 3″

Construct the Block

The instructional photos show the warm colorway.

1. Make 8 copies of the Block 8 foundation paper pattern on vellum.

Use 2 of the extra Center Circle papers cut with Block 4.

2. Refer to Sewing and Appliqué (page 9) to make the Center Circle, the Diamonds, and Wedges.

Special note:

Be sure to position pieces 1 and 2 to the paper so that #2 will cover the space on the paper.

3. Sew together 4 white Block Corners. Sew the round block into the Block Corners. Refer to the photo of the block and *be sure* to orient the round block correctly. The points in the Ring do not line up with the seams in the Corners.

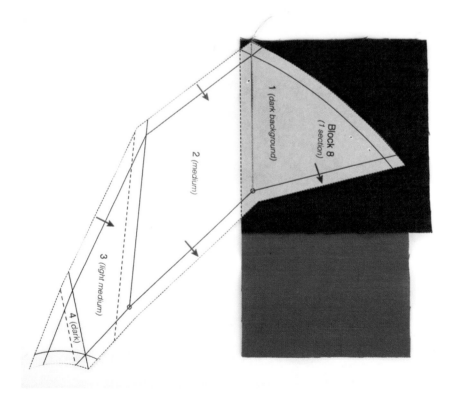

Fabric Cutting: Warm Colorway   *WOF = width of fabric*

CENTER

#	Color (value)	Strips	Individual pieces
1, 3	Fern (medium)	1 @ 2¼″ × WOF	4 @ 2¼″ × 3″
2, 4	Canary (light)	1 @ 2¼″ × WOF	4 @ 2¼″ × 3″

RING SECTION

#	Color (value)	Strips	Individual pieces
1	Iris (dark)	From Block 1	16 @ 4″ × 4″
2	Poppy (dark)	3 @ 3½″ × WOF	16 @ 3½″ × 6½″
3	Peach (light)	3 @ 2″ × WOF	16 @ 2″ × 6″
4	Pomegranate (dark)	2 @ 1¾″ × WOF	16 @ 1¾″ × 3″

4. In this block, the dots on the Center Circle line up *between* points in the Block 8 Ring. The seams also fall between the Ring points.

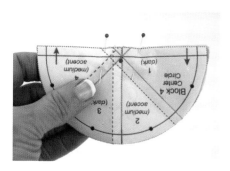
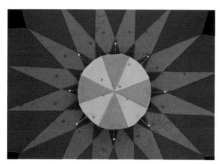

Be sure that the Circle is oriented correctly before you sew it in place.

Place the Center flat on the bed of your sewing machine. Always sew with the Ring on top.

5. Gently press the block from the back, and then from the front. Press the seam allowances toward the Center of the block.

6. Set this block aside until you are ready to finish the quilt.

BLOCK 9
FINISHED BLOCK: 20″ × 20″

Fabric Cutting: Cool Colorway   *WOF = width of fabric*

CENTER

#	Color	Strips	Individual pieces
1, 3	Cornflower blue	1 @ 2¼″ × WOF	4 @ 2¼″ × 3¼″
2, 4	Yellow-green	1 @ 2¼″ × WOF	4 @ 2¼″ × 3¼″

INNER RING

#	Color	Strips	Individual pieces
1	Chartreuse	2 @ 3¼″ × WOF	16 @ 3¼″ × 4″
2	Teal	3 @ 2¼″ × WOF	16 @ 2¼″ × 5½″
3	Lime	2 @ 1¾″ × WOF	16 @ 1¾″ × 3½″

OUTER RING

#	Color (*value*)	Strips	Individual pieces
1, 3	Light aqua	2 @ 3″ × WOF	16 @ 3″ × 4″
2, 4	White	From Block 1	16 @ 4″ × 4″

Construct the Block

The instructional photos show the warm colorway.

1. The foundation paper patterns for Block 9 are on two pages (pages 66 and 67). Make 4 copies of *"page 1"* and 3 copies of *"page 2"* on vellum. Use 2 of the extra Center Circle papers cut with Block 4.

2. Refer to Sewing and Appliqué (page 9) to make the Center Circle, the Diamonds, and Wedges.

Special notes:

• This block has an Inner and Outer Ring and a Center Circle.

• Make 16 Inner Ring Sections and sew them together to make a Ring. Remove the paper from the Inner Ring.

• Make 8 Outer Ring Sections and sew them together to make a Ring. The dots on Outer Ring papers mark spots where you need to match points. Make a light mark on the wrong side of the fabric under each dot before you remove the paper.

Fabric Cutting: Warm Colorway *WOF = width of fabric*

CENTER

#	Color (*value*)	Strips	Individual pieces
1, 3	Carrot (*medium*)	1 @ 2¼˝ × WOF	4 @ 2¼˝ × 3˝
2, 4	Canary (*light*)	1 @ 2¼˝ × WOF	4 @ 2¼˝ × 3˝

INNER RING

#	Color (*value*)	Strips	Individual pieces
1	Shamrock (*dark*)	2 @ 3˝ × WOF	16 @ 3˝ × 4˝
2	Tiger (*medium*)	3 @ 2¼˝ × WOF	16 @ 2¼˝ × 5¼˝
3	Lime (*medium*)	2 @ 1¾˝ × WOF	16 @ 1¾˝ × 3½˝

OUTER RING

#	Color (*value*)	Strips	Individual pieces
1, 3	Peach (*light*)	2 @ 3˝ × WOF	16 @ 3˝ × 4˝
2, 4	Iris (*dark*)	From Block 1	16 @ 4˝ × 4˝

3. Set the Center Circle into the center of the Inner Ring. Press the seam allowances toward the center.

4. Set the Center/Inner Ring into the Outer Ring in the same manner. Use pins to mark the dots to help you match points. Press the seam allowances toward the Outer Ring.

 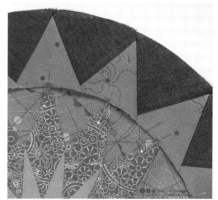

5. Sew together 1 cream and 3 light gray Block Corners. Sew the round block into the Block Corners.

6. Gently press the block from the back, and then from the front. Set this block aside until you are ready to finish the quilt.

SIDE BORDERS

FINISHED SIDE BORDER: 5″ × 60″

Fabric Cutting: Cool Colorway   *WOF = width of fabric*

Set aside excess 1, 2, 3, and 6 fabrics for the top and bottom borders.

#	Color	Strips	Individual pieces
1	Fern	1 @ 4″ × WOF	6 leaves
2, 3	Grass	1 @ 8″ × WOF	6 each—leaves
4, 5	Dark aqua	1 @ 12″ × WOF	6 each—fronds
6	Honey gold	1 @ 2″ × WOF	6 circles

Construct the Side Borders

1. Refer to Appliqué the Borders (page 29) to make 2 Side Borders.

2. Trim away the selvages at the ends of 4 of the border strips that you set aside with Block 1. Sew strips together, end to end, to make 2 Side Border backgrounds 7″ × 62″. Press the seam allowances to one side.

Fabric Cutting: Warm Colorway *WOF = width of fabric*

Set aside excess 1, 2, 3, and 6 fabrics for the top and bottom borders.

#	Color	Strips	Individual pieces
1	Pear	1 @ 4″ × WOF	6 leaves
2, 3	Grass	1 @ 8″ × WOF	6 each—leaves
4, 5	Poppy	1 @ 12″ × WOF	6 each—fronds
6	Beetle blue	1 @ 2″ × WOF	6 circles

Special notes:

- The appliqué shapes come very close to the edges of the border strips. Be careful when you position the pieces and be very careful when you trim the borders after appliqué.

- If you want to make the borders a little wider, trim the side borders to 6″ × 60½″. The side borders will then have a finished width of 5½″. You will need to adjust the width and length of the top/bottom borders. Those measurements are included in the Top/Bottom Border pattern.

TOP/BOTTOM BORDERS
FINISHED TOP AND BOTTOM BORDER: 5˝ × 70˝

Fabric Cutting: Cool Colorway   *WOF = width of fabric*

#	Color	Strips	Individual pieces
1	Light aqua	1 @ 4˝ × WOF	14 leaves
2, 3	Dark aqua	1 @ 8˝ × WOF	14 each—leaves
4, 5	Teal	1 @ 8˝ × WOF	14 each—leaves
6	Dark periwinkle	1 @ 2˝ × WOF	14 circles
7	Fern	From Side Border	12 leaves
8, 9	Grass	From Side Border	12 each—leaves
10	Honey gold	From Side Border	12 circles

Construct the Top and Bottom Borders

1. Refer to Appliqué the Borders (page 29) to make 2 Top and Bottom Borders.

2. Trim away the selvages at the ends of 4 of the border strips that you set aside with Block 1. Sew strips together, end to end, to make 2 Top and Bottom Border backgrounds 7˝ × 72˝. Press the seam allowances to one side.

Fabric Cutting: Warm Colorway   *WOF = width of fabric*

Set aside excess fabrics for the top and bottom borders.

#	Color	Strips	Individual pieces
1	Peach	1 @ 4″ × WOF	14 leaves
2, 3	Tomato	1 @ 8″ × WOF	14 each—leaves
4, 5	Barn	1 @ 8″ × WOF	14 each—leaves
6	Lime	1 @ 2″ × WOF	14 circles
7	Pear	From Side Border	12 leaves
8, 9	Grass	From Side Border	12 each—leaves
10	Beetle blue	From Side Border	12 circles

Special notes:

- The appliqué shapes come very close to the edges of the border strips. Be careful when you position the pieces and be very careful when you trim the borders after appliqué.

- If you made the side borders wider, trim the Top and Bottom Borders to 6″ × 71½″. The borders will then have a finished width of 5½″. The quilt will have a finished size of 71″ × 71″.

- I didn't make a mistake when I attached the bottom border. I like it this way, but you can rotate either border if you wish.

Assembling and Finishing

SET THE QUILT TOGETHER

1. Unfinished blocks should measure 20½″ × 20½″. If they do not, you can trim the blocks to match the smallest block or you can add narrow coping strips to bring them up to size.

Be aware that if you alter the size of the blocks, you will need to alter the sizes of the Outer Borders.

2. Refer to the appropriate quilt assembly diagram and sew the blocks together into rows. Press the seam allowances in alternate directions.

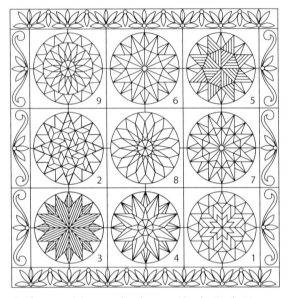

Quilt assembly—cool colorway (*Sizzle Quilt #1*, page 4)

Quilt assembly—warm colorway (*Sizzle Quilt #2*, page 5)

3. Sew the rows together. Press the seam allowances toward the bottom of the quilt.

4. Sew the side borders to the quilt. Press the seam allowances toward the outer borders.

5. Look closely at the orientation of the top and bottom borders, and then sew them to the quilt. Press the seam allowances toward the outer borders.

FINISHING THE QUILT

1. Construct the 80″ × 80″ quilt back, piecing as needed.

2. Place the backing right side down on a firm surface. Tape it down to keep it from moving while you baste.

3. Place the batting over the backing and pat out any wrinkles.

4. Center the quilt top right side up over the batting.

5. Baste the layers together. Yes, I thread baste for both hand and machine quilting. If you like to use safety pins, that's okay too.

6. Quilt by machine or by hand.

7. Trim the outer edges. Leave ¼″ of the backing and batting extending beyond the edge of the quilt top. The extra fabric and batting will fill the binding nicely.

8. Finish the outer edges with continuous bias or straight binding.

9. Attach a hanging sleeve and a label to the back.

Patterns

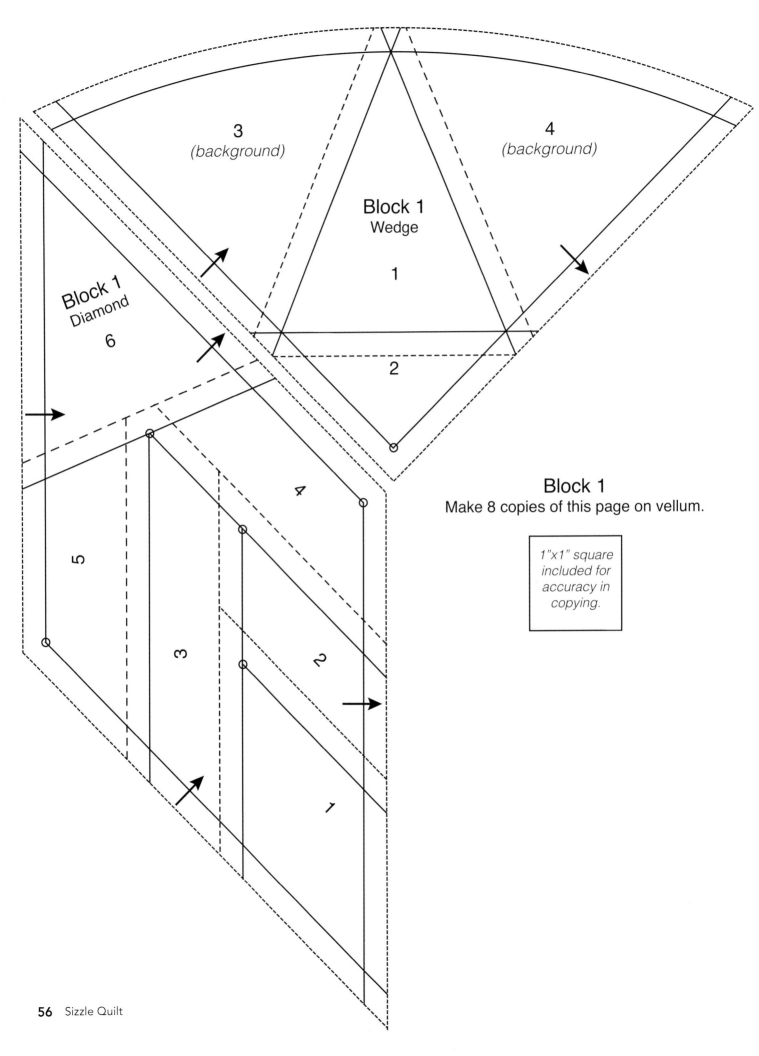

3
(background)

4
(background)

Block 1
Wedge

1

Block 1
Diamond

6

2

Block 1
Make 8 copies of this page on vellum.

1"x1" square included for accuracy in copying.

5

4

3

2

1

Block Corner Template

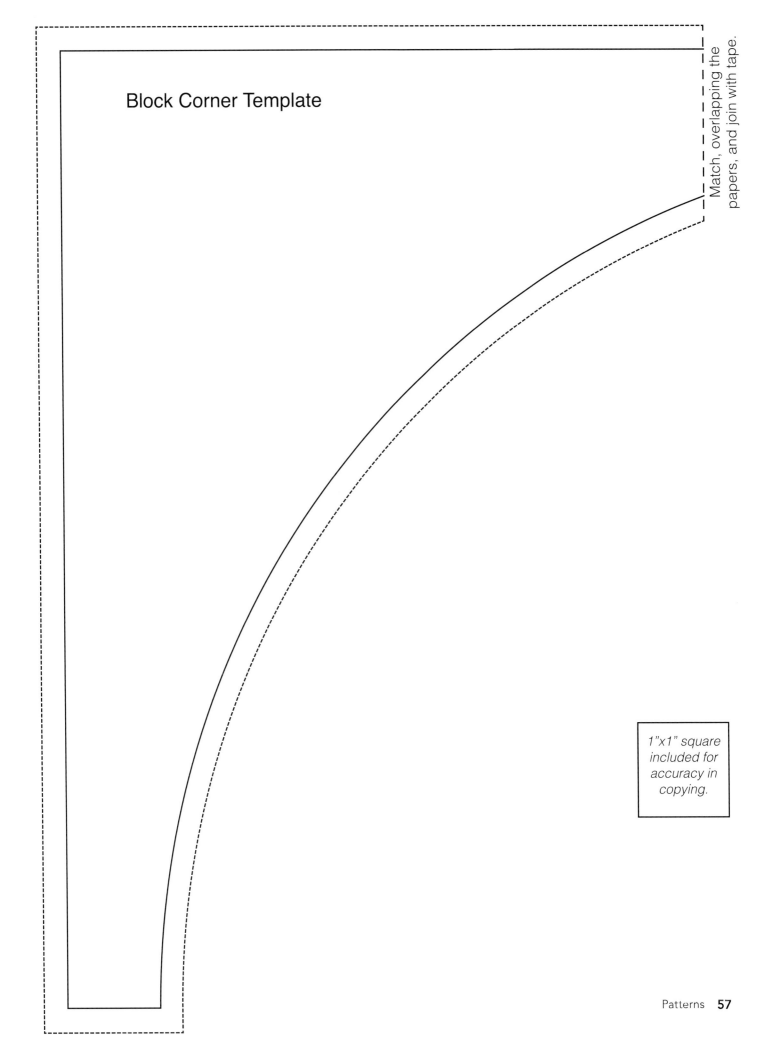

Match, overlapping the papers, and join with tape.

1"x1" square included for accuracy in copying.

Trim and tape to the larger shape.

Cut away excess paper along this line.

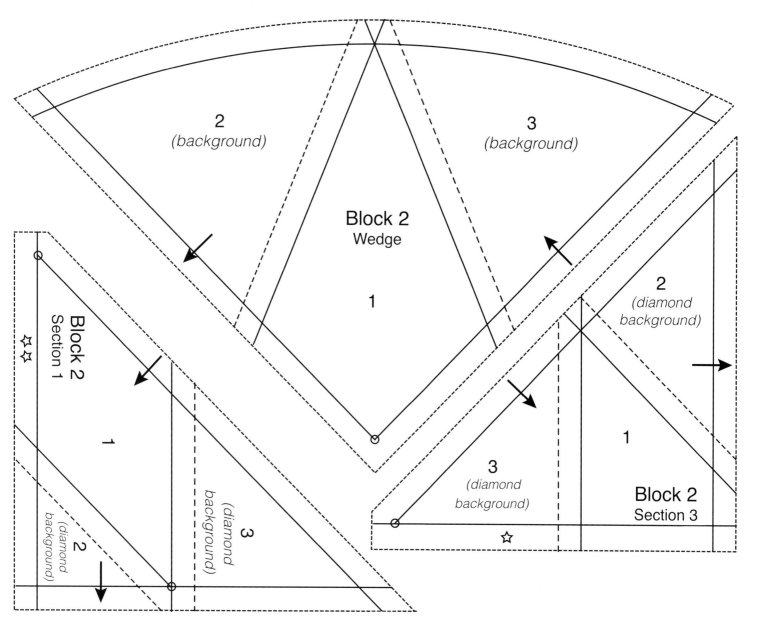

2
(background)

3
(background)

Block 2
Wedge

1

Block 2
Section 1

1

2
(diamond background)

3
(diamond background)

3
(diamond background)

2
(diamond background)

1

Block 2
Section 3

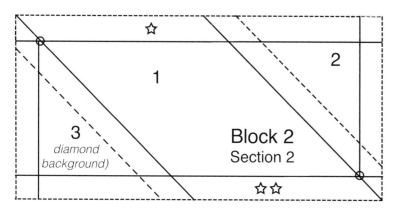

1

2

3
diamond background)

Block 2
Section 2

Block 2
Make 8 copies of this page on vellum.

1"x1" square included for accuracy in copying.

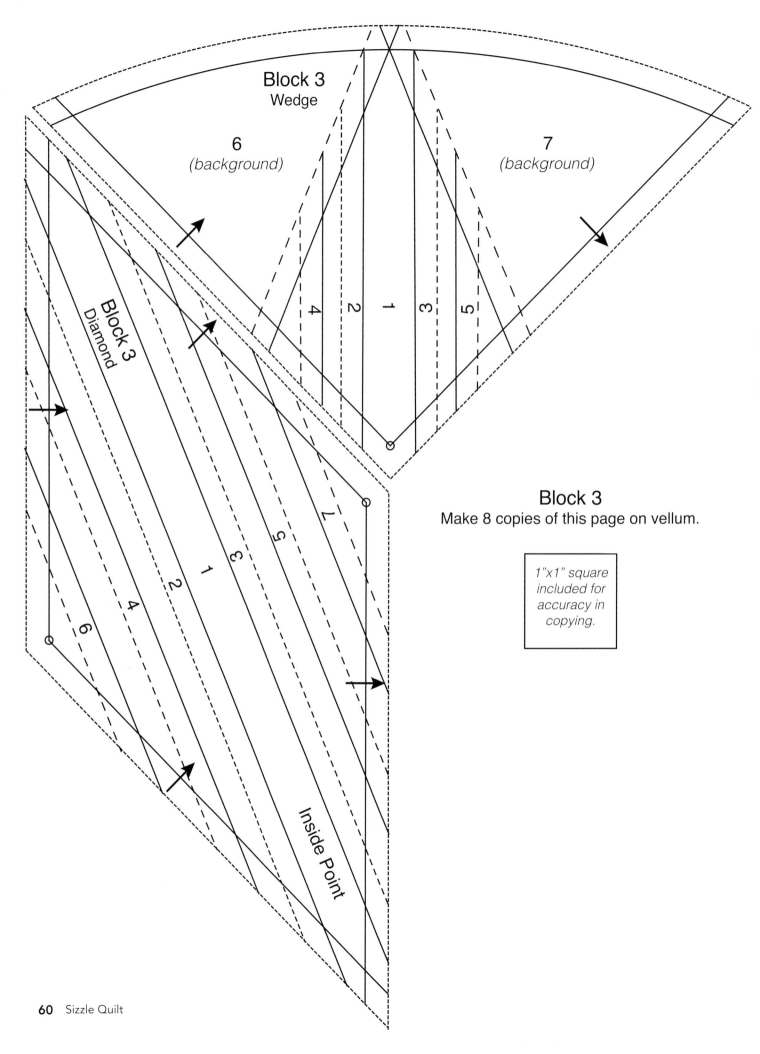

Block 3
Wedge

6
(background)

7
(background)

Block 3
Diamond

Inside Point

Block 3
Make 8 copies of this page on vellum.

1"x1" square
included for
accuracy in
copying.

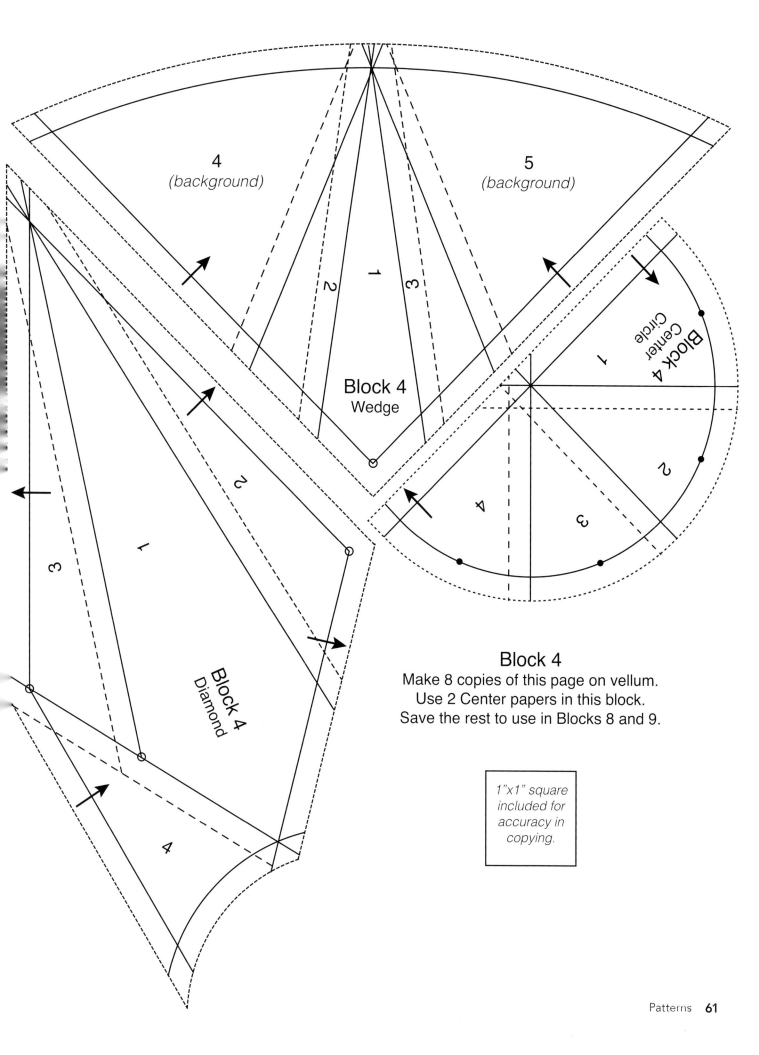

4
(background)

5
(background)

1

2

3

Block 4
Wedge

Block 4
Center Circle

1

2

3

4

3

2

1

4

Block 4
Diamond

Block 4
Make 8 copies of this page on vellum.
Use 2 Center papers in this block.
Save the rest to use in Blocks 8 and 9.

*1"x1" square
included for
accuracy in
copying.*

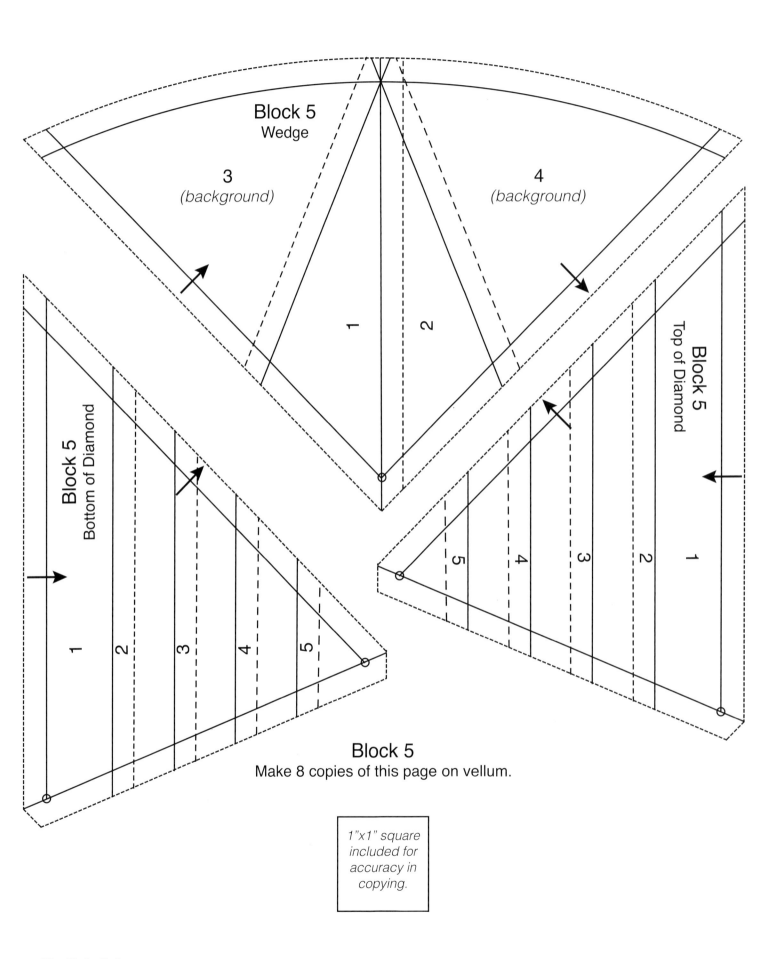

Block 5
Wedge

3
(background)

4
(background)

1

2

Block 5
Bottom of Diamond

Block 5
Top of Diamond

1

2

3

4

5

1

2

3

4

5

Block 5
Make 8 copies of this page on vellum.

1"x1" square
included for
accuracy in
copying.

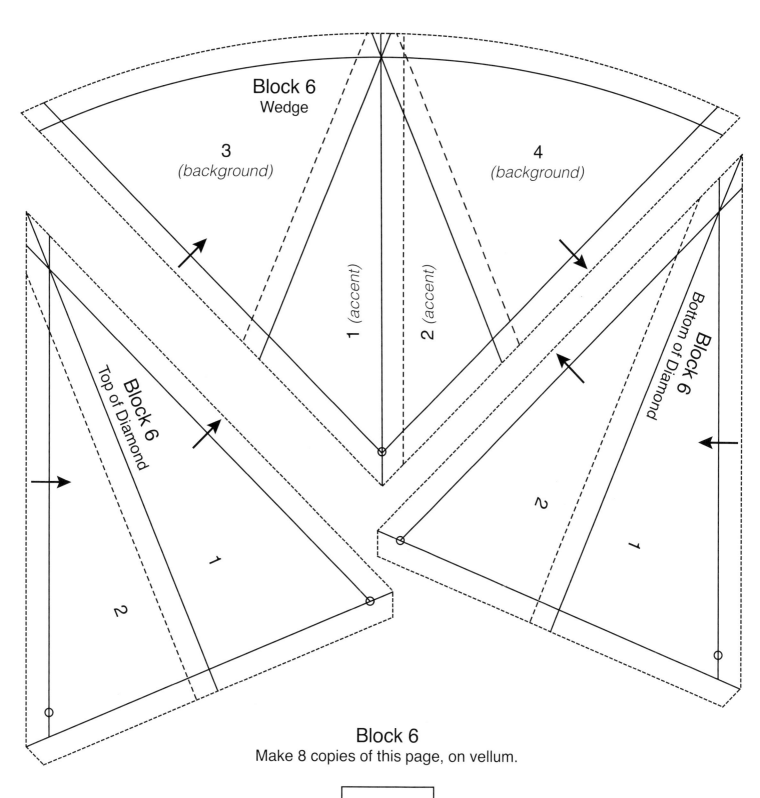

Block 6
Wedge

3
(background)

4
(background)

1 *(accent)*

2 *(accent)*

Block 6
Top of Diamond

1

2

Block 6
Bottom of Diamond

2

1

Block 6
Make 8 copies of this page, on vellum.

*1"x1" square
included for
accuracy in
copying.*

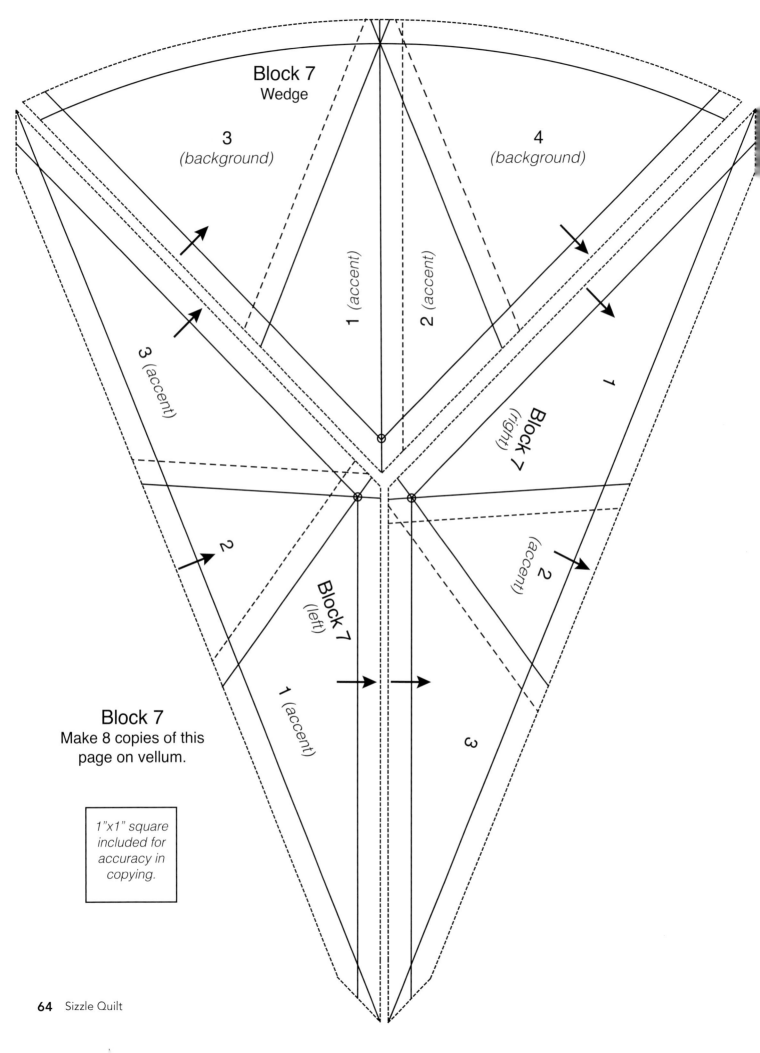

Block 7
Wedge

3
(background)

4
(background)

1 (accent)

2 (accent)

3 (accent)

Block 7
(right)

1

2
(accent)

2

Block 7
(left)

1 (accent)

3

Block 7
Make 8 copies of this
page on vellum.

1"x1" square
included for
accuracy in
copying.

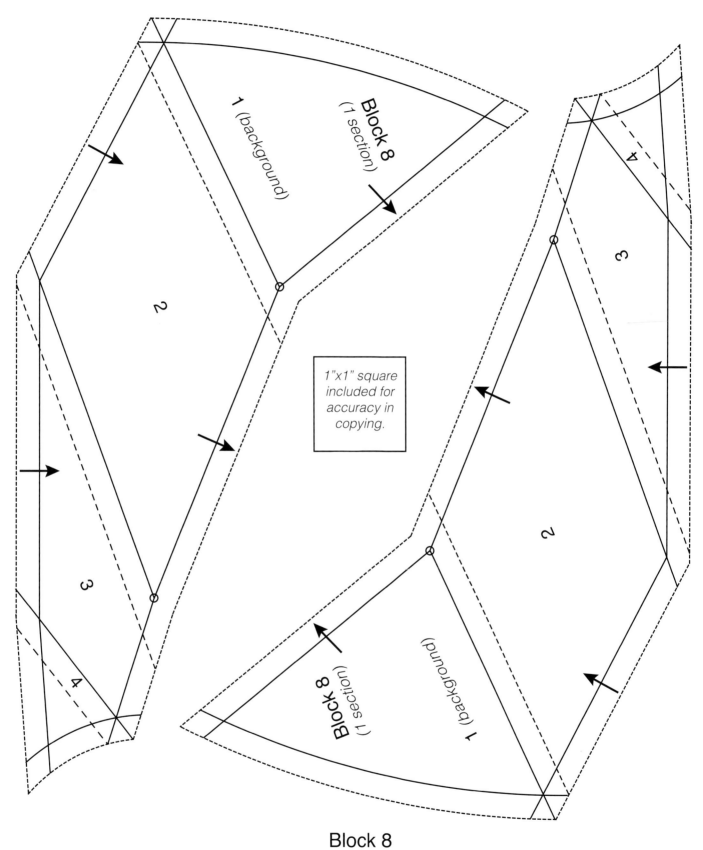

1 (background)

Block 8
(1 section)

2

1"x1" square
included for
accuracy in
copying.

3

4

3

4

2

Block 8
(1 section)

1 (background)

Block 8
Make 8 copies of this page on vellum.
Use 2 of the extra Center papers saved from Block 4.

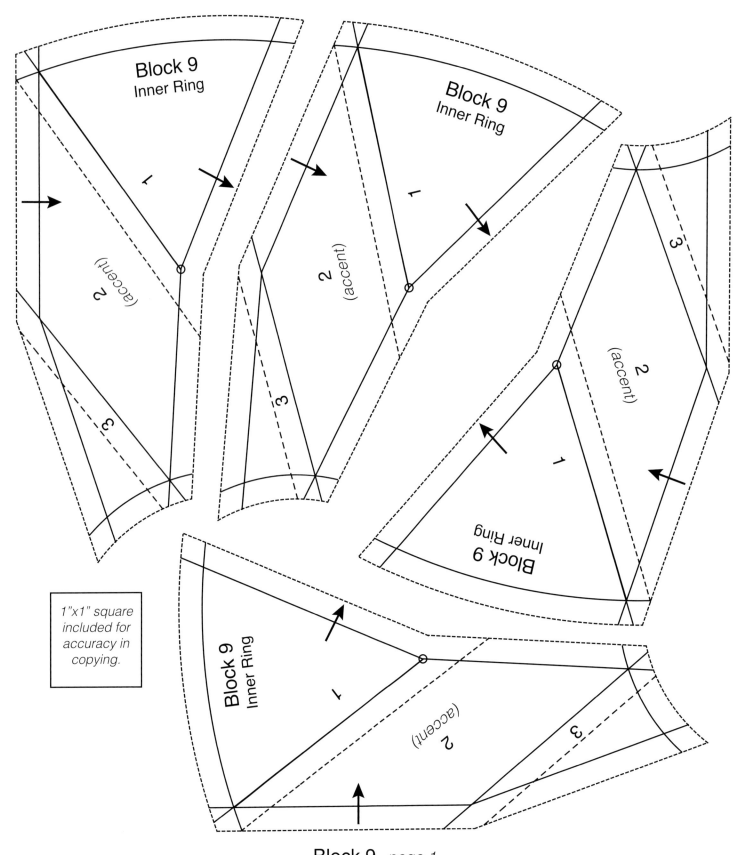

Block 9
Inner Ring

Block 9
Inner Ring

Block 9
Inner Ring

Block 9
Inner Ring

1
2
(accent)
3

1
2
(accent)
3

1
2
(accent)
3

1
2
(accent)
3

1"x1" square included for accuracy in copying.

Block 9, *page 1*
Make 4 copies of this page on vellum.
Use 2 of the extra Center papers saved from Block 4.

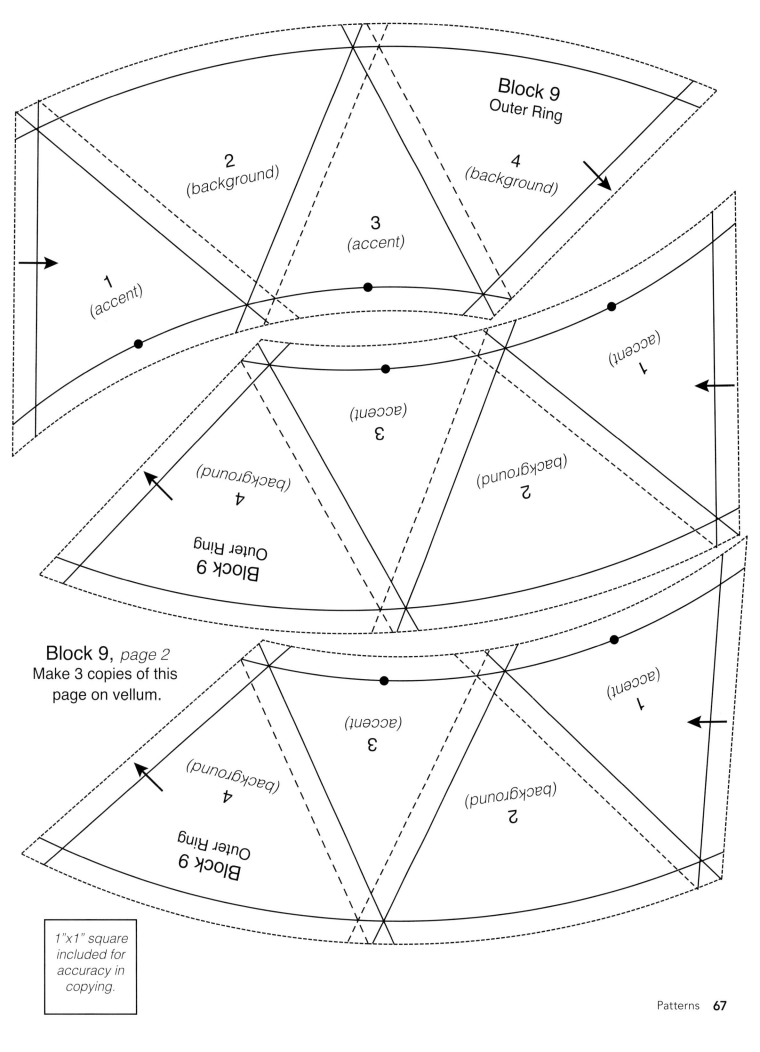

Block 9
Outer Ring

2
(background)

4
(background)

3
(accent)

1
(accent)

3
(accent)

1
(accent)

4
(background)

Block 9
Outer Ring

2
(background)

Block 9, *page 2*
Make 3 copies of this
page on vellum.

3
(accent)

1
(accent)

4
(background)

Block 9
Outer Ring

2
(background)

*1"x1" square
included for
accuracy in
copying.*

Side Border

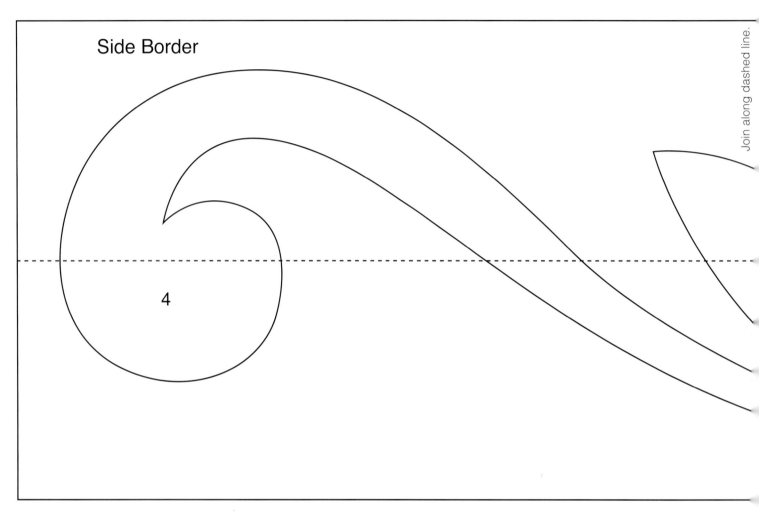

4

Side Border
Page 1

Make 3 copies of this page.
Trim and tape together Side Border pages 1-3 to make three 5″ x 20″ border segments.
Tape the segments together end-to-end to make one 5″ x 60″ Side Border pattern.

*1″x1″ square
included for
accuracy in
copying.*

Side Border

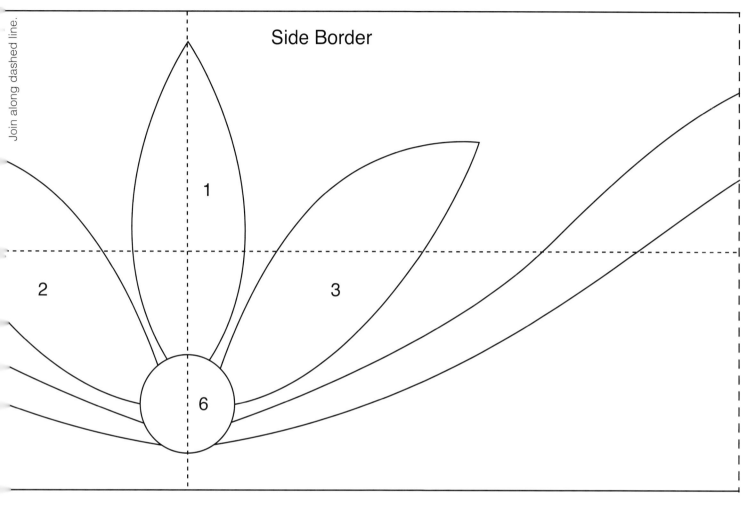

Side Border
Page 2

Make 3 copies of this page.
Trim and tape together Side Border pages 1-3 to make three 5″ x 20″ border segments.
Tape the segments together end-to-end to make one 5″ x 60″ Side Border pattern.

*1″x1″ square
included for
accuracy in
copying.*

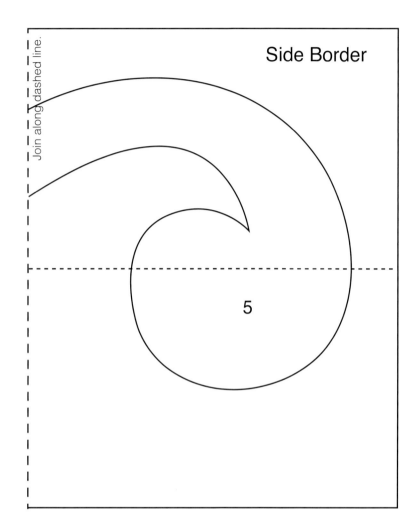

Side Border

Join along dashed line.

5

Side Border
Page 3

Make 3 copies of this page.
Trim and tape together Side Border pages 1-3 to make three 5″ x 20″ border segments.
Tape the segments together end-to-end to make one 5″ x 60″ Side Border pattern.

*1″x1″square
included for
accuracy in
copying.*

Side Border Templates
Make 6 copies on *Quilter's Freezer Paper Sheets* or trace by hand onto freezer paper on a roll.

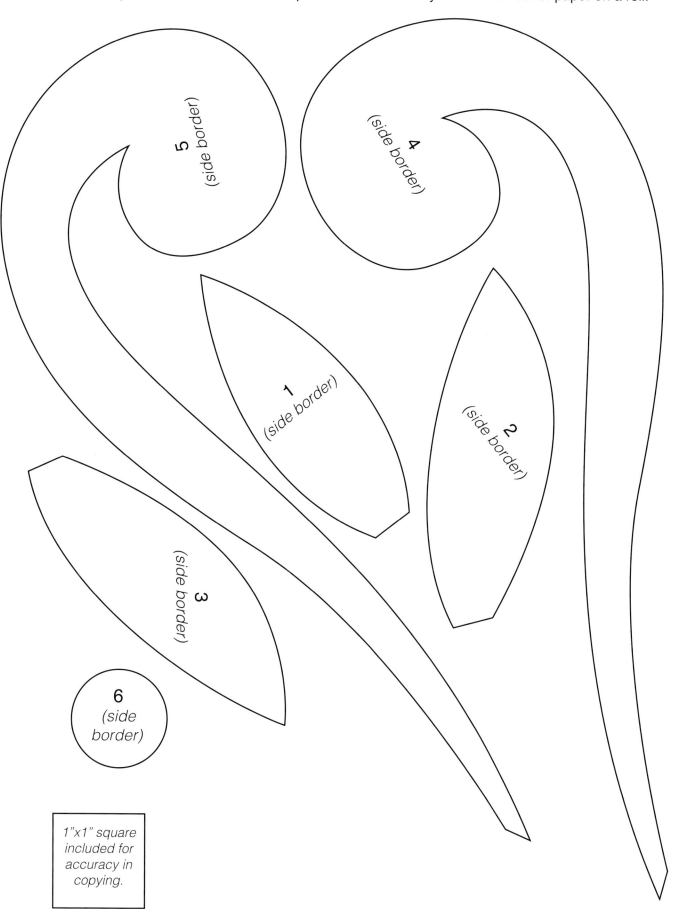

5
(side border)

4
(side border)

1
(side border)

2
(side border)

3
(side border)

6
(side border)

1"x1" square included for accuracy in copying.

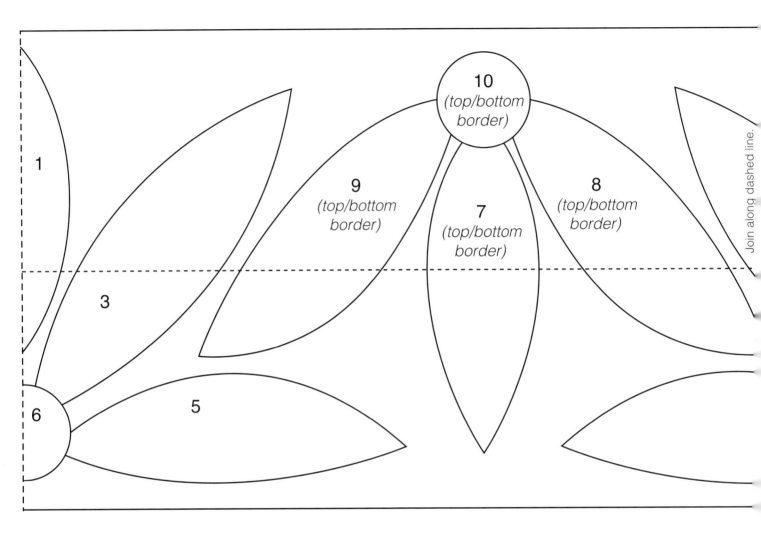

Join along dashed line.

Top/Bottom Border
Page 1

Make 3 copies of this page.
Trim and tape together Top/Bottom Border pages 1-3 to make three 5″ x 20″ border segments.
Tape the segments together end-to-end to make one 5″ x 60″ border pattern.
Trim and tape the Left and Right Sides to the ends of the strip to complete
the 5″ x 70″ Top/Bottom Border pattern.

*1″x1″square
included for
accuracy in
copying.*

Top/Bottom Border

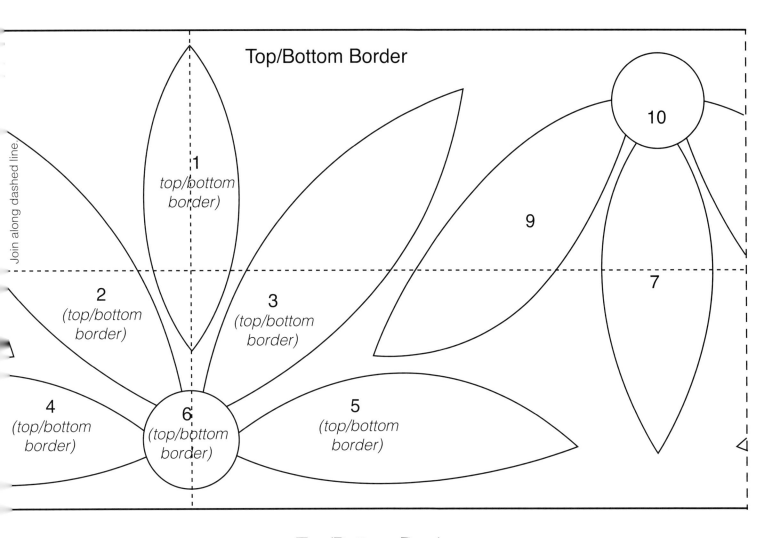

Join along dashed line.

1 top/bottom border)

2 (top/bottom border)

3 (top/bottom border)

4 (top/bottom border)

6 (top/bottom border)

5 (top/bottom border)

9

10

7

Top/Bottom Border
Page 2

Make 3 copies of this page.
Trim and tape together Top/Bottom Border pages 1-3 to make three 5″ x 20″ border segments.
Tape the segments together end-to-end to make one 5″ x 60″ border pattern.
Trim and tape the Left and Right Sides to the ends of the strip to complete
the 5″ x 70″ Top/Bottom Border pattern.

1″x1″ square included for accuracy in copying.

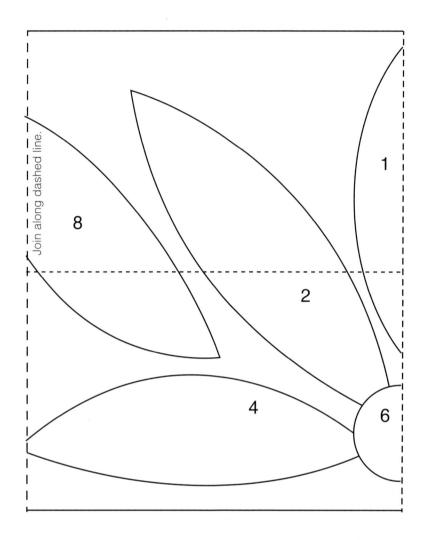

Join along dashed line.

Top/Bottom Border
Page 3

Make 3 copies of this page.
Trim and tape together Top/Bottom Border pages 1-3 to make three 5″ x 20″ border segments.
Tape the segments together end-to-end to make one 5″ x 60″ border pattern.
Trim and tape the Left and Right Sides to the ends of the strip to complete
the 5″ x 70″ Top/Bottom Border pattern.

*1″x1″square
included for
accuracy in
copying.*

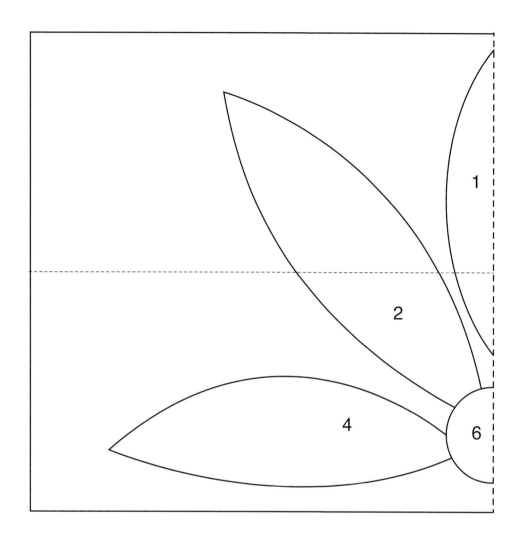

Top/Bottom Border - Left Side

Make 1 copy of this page.
Trim and tape the Left Side to the left end of the pattern strip to complete
the 5˝ x 70˝ Top/Bottom Border pattern.

*1˝x1˝ square
included for
accuracy in
copying.*

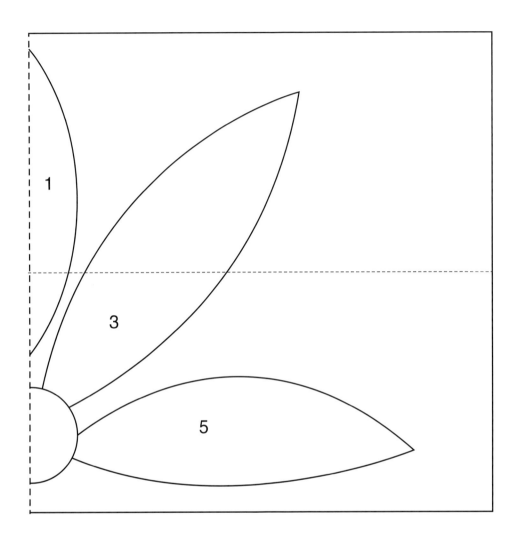

Top/Bottom Border - Right Side

Make 1 copy of this page.
Trim and tape the Right Side to the left end of the pattern strip to complete
the 5″ x 70″ Top/Bottom Border pattern.

*1˝x1˝ square
included for
accuracy in
copying.*

Top/Bottom Border Templates

Make 7 copies on *Quilter's Freezer Paper Sheets* or trace by hand onto freezer paper on a roll.

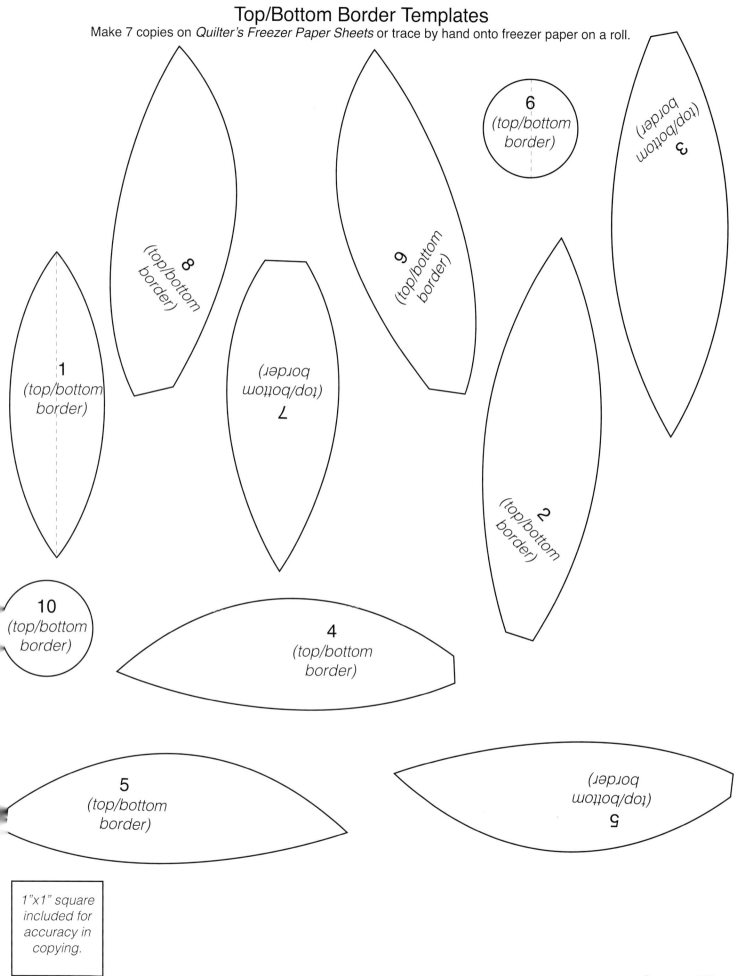

6
(top/bottom border)

8
(top/bottom border)

9
(top/bottom border)

3
(top/bottom border)

1
(top/bottom border)

7
(top/bottom border)

2
(top/bottom border)

10
(top/bottom border)

4
(top/bottom border)

5
(top/bottom border)

5
(top/bottom border)

1"x1" square included for accuracy in copying.

Top/Bottom Border Templates
Make 7 copies on *Quilter's Freezer Paper Sheets* or trace by hand onto freezer paper on a roll.

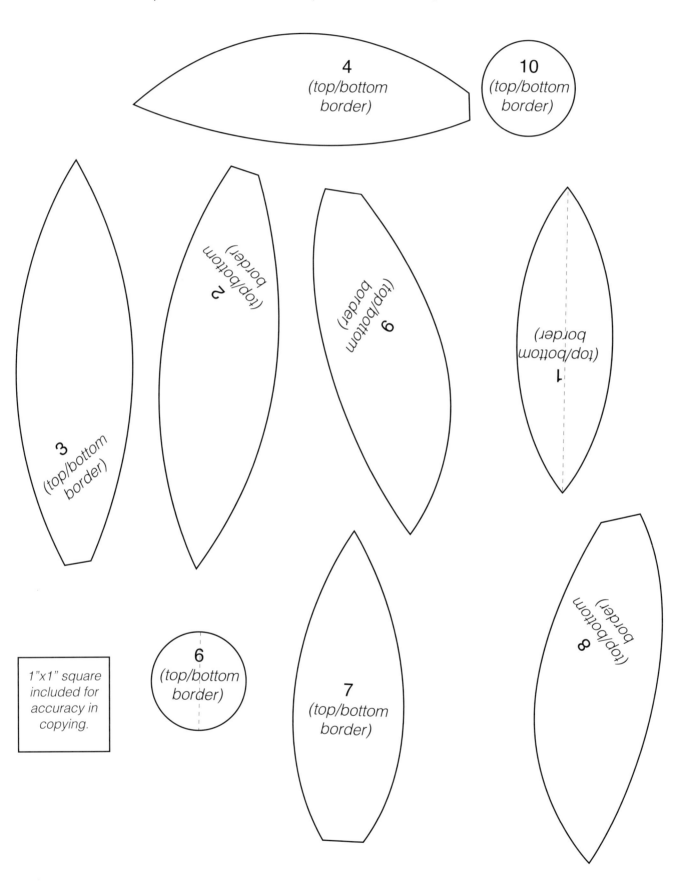

4
(top/bottom border)

10
(top/bottom border)

2
(top/bottom border)

9
(top/bottom border)

1
(top/bottom border)

3
(top/bottom border)

8
(top/bottom border)

6
(top/bottom border)

7
(top/bottom border)

1"x1" square included for accuracy in copying.

About the Author

Becky Goldsmith began quilting in 1986. She and Linda Jenkins formed Piece O' Cake Designs in 1994. Becky has found that designing and making quilts, and teaching others how to make quilts, is a better career than she could ever have imagined.

Quilters are wonderful people, and Becky loves being a part of the global quilt world. She wants to thank you for including her in your quilting life!

Visit Becky online and follow on social media!

Website: pieceocake.com

Blog: pieceocakeblog.com

Facebook: /becky.goldsmith.poc

Pinterest: /pieceocake

Instagram: @beckygoldsmith

Twitter: @beckygoldsmith

YouTube: /beckygoldsmith

Also by Becky Goldsmith:

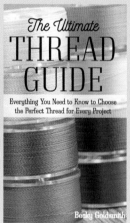

BONUS VIDEOS

*For video tutorials about the Sizzle Quilt blocks and more,
visit C&T Publishing's YouTube channel:*

youtube.com/candtpublishing > search "Sizzle Quilt"